GARLAND STUDIES IN

AMERICAN POPULAR HISTORY AND CULTURE

edited by

JEROME NADELHAFT
UNIVERSITY OF MAINE

A GARLAND SERIES

LOLITA IN PEYTON PLACE

HIGHBROW, MIDDLEBROW, AND LOWBROW NOVELS OF THE 1950s

RUTH PIRSIG WOOD

GARLAND PUBLISHING, Inc.
NEW YORK & LONDON / 1995

Library of Congress Cataloging-in-Publication Data

Wood, Ruth Persig, 1945–
    Lolita in Peyton Place : highbrow, middlebrow, and lowbrow
novels of the 1950s / Ruth Persig Wood
        p.   cm. — (Garland studies in American popular history
and culture)
    Includes bibliographical references and index.
    ISBN 0-8153-2061-2 (alk. paper)
    1. American fiction—20th century—history and criticism.
2. Popular literature—United States—History—20th century.
3. Moral conditions in literature. 4. Ethics in literature.
5. Literature and society—United States—History—20th century.
6. Best sellers—United States—Bibliography. 7. Books and reading—United States—History. 8. Social values in literature. 9. Sex
roles in literature. I. Title. II. Series.
PS374.P63W66 1995
813'.5409—dc20   95-22338

To my husband,
David Wood

CONTENTS

PREFACE

RAISING MY BROWS

Some people look at films like *Home Alone II*, tune in to MTV, or watch Robert James Waller top the bestseller lists for endless months and worry that Western civilization is about to collapse. I'm not one of them. Some of my best friends are pop culture junkies, and I work with America's youth, so I want better reasons before I blame anything on the television age and, particularly, on "pulp fiction."

My inclination is not well supported by critical inquiry. Even Janice Radway, who set out to support women's reading of romances, couldn't go as far as she wanted in that defense. One can find support of a somewhat sensational kind from the likes of Camille Paglia, Stephen King, and the various defenders of pornography.

But much of the commentary on popular fiction doesn't go far beyond description; that which does is largely censorious. I'm aware that my subtitle may sound like I'm getting ready to fulminate as well. I'm not. Though I agree with C.S. Lewis that "lowbrow," "middlebrow" and "highbrow" are "odious adjectives," I decided to use them because the alternatives I considered sounded equally pejorative, snobbish, and smug. The offensive denotations at least emphasize the need for a reconsideration. Those who see justice in the pejorative "low" and the laudatory "high" are just the ones I want to engage in a reconsideration.

My purpose is to provide sounder theoretical reasons for not only allowing, but even advocating the consumption of popular fiction in schools, by women, in society at large. This study involves an attempt to discern and discuss the redeeming qualities of the nonliterary or popular American fiction of the fifties.

I quickly realized that I needed more than the common two-part division between "pop fiction" and "literature." There is a body of popular fiction ("middlebrow") which focuses on character in relation to society, has the basic structure and function of myth, and often appeals to readers of either sex. Another kind ("lowbrow"), is usually read by members of one sex, focuses on character in relation to a narrow circle (one other individual or a closed group), follows the plot patterns of romance or fairy tale, and implies how to be a "good man" or a "good woman."

These forms have different generic make-up and serve different cultural and readerly functions. To critique them successfully, we need to know more about what they aim for and how they're constructed. So part of my goal is to show how the differences between these subgenres should lead us to apply different standards of critical judgment. The three-part taxonomy seems useful for finding out what lowbrow and middlebrow fictions contribute to culture that highbrow can't, why some lowbrow and middlebrow novels are better than others, and how lowbrow, middlebrow, and highbrow connect variously to history, ideology, and sociology.

Highbrow novels are those distinguished by an author's conscious striving toward artistry and the absence of model characters or moral centers. One surprise for me in this study is that highbrow novels are more like lowbrow novels than like middlebrow. Readers in the last century have tended to be much more aware of the differences than the similarities. Though detached and ironized in tone and relation to audience, highbrow novels are like lowbrow in form and function. I discuss those similarities in chapters one and seven, and in chapter eight I examine reasons why trained readers are easily repelled by lowbrow fiction as well as reasons why we shouldn't be.

Chapter four details the generic differences; chapter five discusses how the three levels serve different cultural functions. Chapters six and seven discuss how they serve different individual needs. Chapter two explains why a "quintessential" fifties novel has to be "middlebrow."

The taxonomy is derived from American fiction of the fifties and therefore holds true for work from that time and place more than for any other time or place. The appendix, entitled "The Fifties," gives an overview of the dominant social, historical, ideological, and economic features of this decade that I see as influencing the themes and morals of American fifties fiction. This study has made clearer to me that the cultural artifacts that we regard as good and appropriate entertainment influence the way we train ourselves to view each other, the world, and our places in it.

Genres evolve to serve cultural needs; chapter three examines how major historical, economic, and social changes influenced the evolution of fictional genres. In the fifties we made different decisions about human issues than we do now. For that reason, and because of changes in our economy, modes of interaction, and social realities, the novel forms that currently appear on bestseller lists don't exactly match the forms of lowbrow, middlebrow, and highbrow novels I describe here. Lowbrow novels like *The Bridges of Madison County* have reformulated the definition of "good man" and "good woman" to suit the ethics of the time, and we've evolved hybrids of low-middlebrow (Grisham and Crichton, for example) and low-highbrow (Erdrich and Morrison, for example). But that's the subject of my next book.

All the titles of popular fiction that get discussed at any length in this book appeared on national bestseller lists in the fifties or early sixties. That system of selection pretty much eliminated *real* "pulp fiction." I also chose to omit less realistic subgenres—sagas, historical romances, science fiction, and fantasy—in order to make more parallel comparisons. For the sake of expediency (since in this age of the VCR it's safer to assume familiarity with popular movies than with popular fiction), I've used some eighties and nineties films for comparative purposes.

I'd like to thank Professor Kent Bales for giving me encouragement to explore this topic in the variety of directions it led me. I'd like to thank my husband, Dave Wood, who has been my primary editor and moral support from beginning to end, and Dick Parker, who has ably steered me through the final stages. I'd also like to thank my editors at Garland who have been very "lowbrow" to deal with. That's a compliment.

Ruth Pirsig Wood
Minneapolis, Minnesota
April 1995

Lolita in *Peyton Place*

I

LOLITA IN *PEYTON PLACE*

Readers who regard Vladimir Nabokov's *Lolita* as lewd vulgarity cleverly disguised as an art novel may be pleased with this chapter's premise that *Lolita* is remarkably similar to Grace Metalious's *Peyton Place*. Those who regard *Lolita* as elevating art and *Peyton Place* as titillating potboiler may abhor the comparison. I suggest it not to tease or titillate, but to challenge some common assumptions about how "high" and "low" fiction differ.

We tend to categorize novels by what they look like and whom they appeal to rather than by their structures, techniques, and functions. These two novels have been packaged and received as very different sorts, one that excites and evades, one that illuminates and challenges. Yet they make, I will argue, very similar statements.

I am not proposing that we reconsider the *quality* of these novels, but that we revise our tactics of evaluation. Under different lenses, the novels have much in common. Both are stories of a pubescent girl's matriculation to womanhood.[1] Both lay bare the hazards of that process: abandonment, rejection, overprotection, underprotection, victimization. Both heroines transcend into womanhood (Lolita has to die in childbirth to get there; nonetheless, she is transcendent).

Peyton Place focuses on Allison MacKenzie, an unhappy, fatherless twelve-year-old bewildered by her peers' interest in boys. Her mother, Constance, is determined to spare Allison her own blemished fate of bearing a "bastard" child. The story follows Allison through the beginning of her career when she submits to fate and the attentions of her married New York editor. In the novel's "happy" ending, she welcomes romantic overtures from a man of more appropriate age and marital status—David Noyes (a name in which no yields to yes).[2]

While Allison is something of a Little Red Riding Hood seen

3

through Granny's eyes, Lolita is that same character seen by the wolf. She, too, is a fatherless twelve-year-old controlled by a conventional mother, Charlotte Haze. Her unhappiness and bewilderment become known through Humbert's occasional admissions—that Lolita began their affair with a child's skewed notion of what sexuality amounts to, that once she's given herself to Humbert, she cries every night when she thinks Humbert has fallen asleep, and that she believes that Humbert "broke her life."[3] She is seventeen at the novel's end, great with child, and happily married to a "lamb" of a husband, Dick Schiller.

The victimization is straightforward in *Lolita*—partly the result of Charlotte's stupid self-interest, for she marries Humbert despite his evident lack of interest in her, and she fails to recognize Lolita's precocity as anything but bratty impertinence. Perverted Humbert thus gains access to "nymphet" Lolita. And, when Charlotte is killed by an incredibly convenient wayward auto, Humbert compounds his opportunity by lying to Lolita, plying her with gifts, and drugging her into a compliant sleep.

The victimization in *Peyton Place* is "displaced." Vladimir Propp explains that various standard plot functions and characters can be represented in a variety of ways—by having the standard one replaced by a metonymic substitute. This is sometimes accomplished by having one character "split in two" or using one to perform two functions.[4]

Her best friend, Selina (whose name is an anagram of Allison) is the metonymic double—Allison's sexual and more vulnerable self. It is Selina who must suffer sexual assault by her stepfather, Lucas Cross. And that victimization is caused in part by the mother's deficient vigilance. Though she knew he "always drank and fought and chased wimmin," Nellie married Lucas shortly after Selina's father had been killed because she was "alone . . . and Lucas was after [her]" (156).

Both novels traffic in time-worn notions of the treacherous journey into adulthood and "sins of the fathers." Lolita is cast adrift with two tainted parents in an unsupportive world. Charlotte's "harlot" desire for sexual consummation with the handsome humbug distracts her from attending to her daughter's needs, and Humbert has had a childhood which, by his own account, mangled his abilities to function normally.

Lolita appears to have no support system, and no one seems capable of imagining what Humbert is actually doing. Quilty, a playwright who has the same designs on Lolita, is the only person who recognizes Humbert's relationship with Lolita for what it is.[5]

The cross-country ramble from motel to motel frees Humbert and

Lolita from the morality of the flock. In short, the mobility, individuality, isolation of mid-twentieth century American life enable Humbert to have his way with Lolita and provide her little alternative (as Humbert often reminds her) to submitting to his demands; there is no woodsman to rescue her.[6]

In *Peyton Place*, New York City symbolizes the anonymous inattentiveness of modern America, for it is here that both Allison and her mother have sexual relationships with married men. Selina is victimized by another kind of inattentiveness—of a mother frequently absent from the home or so hopelessly drunk when she is there that the stepfather may willfully act out his indecent urges. Furthermore, the Cross family lives in "shanty town," outside the watchful community, beyond the range of schoolteacher Elsie Thornton's symbolic gaze from upper story schoolroom windows. No woodsman for Selina either.

The "sins of the fathers" are represented in numerous cases of repressive parenting in Peyton Place. For example, Selina's boyfriend, Ted Carter, turns out to be more self-serving than magnanimous as he refuses to volunteer to fight in World War II and to stand by Selina when she is tried for her father's murder. The novel suggests that this behavior is genetically determined. Ted was born of parents so self-serving that even after they were engaged, they agreed that his mother should first marry a sickly rich old man, so that the two of them could later live luxuriously off her inheritance.

In terms of time-worn sexual ethics, the two novels give reflexive accounts of the same moral concern: the effects of sexual self-indulgence and of sexual repression. The ill effects of both are illustrated by Rodney Harrington and Norman Page in *Peyton Place*; in *Lolita* by Humbert. Rodney is the scion of the town's wheeler-dealer, Leslie Harrington,[7] who believes that in order to become the kind of man he wants him to be Rodney must indulge his male prerogatives. Three of those converge—driving fast, drinking hard, and using women—when a drunken Rodney causes a fatal auto wreck while fondling his date's breasts.

Norman's widowed mother believes that Norman, even in his mid-teens, should not think about the opposite sex; whatever anxiety he experiences is best relieved by giving him an enema. Norman's trained fear of reality results—at least as Metalious suggests—in his becoming effeminate and cowardly.

Humbert Humbert is part Norman, part Rodney. He sees his unconsummated love affair with Annabelle Leigh when they were both twelve as the source of his obsession with nymphets. Adult interference stymied two attempts at a love-making that Humbert thought would have been entirely natural and mutually gratifying. He explains that because he was not able to take what he wanted when it was appropriate to do so he is forever seduced by the forbidden and dissatisfied with what is socially sanctioned (Charlotte, for instance). This is his own Lacanian analysis of being "enslaved in desire" by primal repression.[8]

As an adult blessed with an unearned income and sexy good looks, Humbert compensates by acquiring a raft of sexual partners. He dispatches most of them with little regret, for they are prostitutes or women of such little self-esteem that Humbert feels they expect to be dumped by the time he dumps them. Charlotte poses more of a problem. Humbert acknowledges that if he were a more normal man, Charlotte would have been an adequate wife.[9] Humbert's guilt for "crushing" her when she learns of his interest in Lolita is displaced onto the wayward auto.

Humbert's Norman and Rodney converge in his relationship with Lolita. Though he professes to be "strangulated" by his own taboos (20) and anxious to preserve his "inner essential innocence" (273), Humbert's best intentions are undone when circumstances facilitate access to Lolita. At first, he convinces himself that if he can achieve orgasm without coitus—which happens one Sunday when Charlotte is at church and he strokes Lolita's thigh as she lies on the couch—or penetrate her only when she is drugged beyond consciousness, he can satisfy his craving for Lolita without harming her; i.e., if she is "solipsized," he can "enjoy her" (57). He resorts to citing historical and literary precedent for the normalcy of mature males mating with pubescent females (20-1), but none are from contemporary American culture or even the modern era. Thus his rapture at possessing Lolita is everywhere tempered with the anxiety that he has ruined her childhood, that Lolita would always prefer something other than what he prefers, that she never achieves orgasm, that she cries herself to sleep.

Still, he never thinks of providing a more normal life for her, again because of his double nature: part of him needs her too much, part of him fears exposure and incarceration. Humbert becomes trapped in the relationship as much as Lolita is imprisoned by him. He can only give up his obsession after Lolita has become a pregnant housewife, when he finally realizes that their relationship had been for her "a bit of dry mud caking her childhood" (248).

His idealized version of life with Lolita thus contrasts with the actuality of it as Allison's story contrasts with Selina's. In Josipovici's terms, "Humbert tries to possess carnally what can only be possessed in the imagination" (46). Salomon says that this "temporal dissonance"— the gap between life and art—is the novel's theme (216). For Humbert to survive this revelation he must achieve some middle ground of reconciliation between reality and imagination or between life and art.

Their differing ways of reconciling what the imagination desires and the world allows make these examples of lowbrow and highbrow novels seem "poles apart." Nabokov makes it clear that reconciliation is a "figment of the pen," while Metalious makes no such concessions. For his admission, Nabokov is seen as a truth-teller; for her concupiscence Metalious appears destructively false. Yet what they offer as reconciliation and what they do with their material are not so fundamentally different.

In playing the truth-teller, Nabokov frequently reminds us that we're "reading *words*" (44). Patricia Merivale says, "Nabokov never lets his reader forget that he is the conjuror, the illusionist, the stage manager, to whom his characters owe their existence."[10] Early in the novel Humbert says to no one in particular, "Darling this is only a game" (21). Pryce-Jones remarks that Nabokov is "all the time observing himself at work, knocking down . . . the very page that he's been at pains to construct" (69).

Drawing attention to fictive construction curbs the emotional pain of unfulfilled desire by detaching readers from the fates of made-up characters, without denying the poignancy of the desire. The antidote to despair in *Lolita* is not in ostensibly closing the gap, as in *Peyton Place*, but in continuing to "desire the closure."[11]

Desire stays alive in this novel because Humbert is cast into the role of story-teller or bard, whose personal whims rather than the workings of fate, God, or society, inscribe the story. Art itself becomes the middle ground in *Lolita* by providing a way for Humbert to both have Lolita and clear the caking mud. If this book becomes Humbert's Grecian Urn with maids "forever young, forever wanting," then Humbert's loss of Lolita is not entirely tragic. As Keats's ode suggests, it is more thrilling to want than to possess.

Possession involves a contract, and a contract involves compromise. An additional aspect of highbrow novels which I'll take up in chapter four is a distrust or downright fear of "mutual" love relationships. The traditional dictum that "two shall be as one" means an automatic loss of autonomy. This truism helps explain why women in romance novels so relish the married state, since they have no autonomy to lose, and why detectives marry their secretaries and doctors their nurses: to find partners who will not compromise their own personal goals.

Humbert manages to put the pieces of himself together without marriage and without denying his "inner essential innocence." He denies his separation from Lolita by denying that she existed, and he denies his own lust by killing Quilty. Apotheosized into an eternally young yet fecund earth mother, Lolita is made both fictive and renewable by her death in childbirth. Having "contained" his guilt of *using* Lolita for only lustful purposes in the doppelganger Quilty,[12] Humbert is made innocent by Quilty's death.

Nabokov's inventive flamboyance in "wiping out" characters who interfere with fulfillment of desire is a mark of self-conscious high-brow style. Metalious (with less élan) is as energetic an expunger. Selina gets away with murdering her stepfather when local doctor Matt Swain (a protective surrogate father, the inverse of Lucas Cross) steps forward to testify that he aborted the fetus that Lucas had planted in Selina. Swain's impeccable reputation deters anyone's pressing charges against him, so Cross is dispatched without an echo.

The appearance of Allison's father would complicate Constance's chances at reclamation, but he has died an early and unexplained death (conveniently leaving money for Constance). Like her father, Allison's lover melds into the "otherness" of New York City; Ted Carter fades from the scene as a self-absorbed college boy; Norman goes to a sanitarium; Nellie hangs herself when she learns of Lucas's incest.

The big difference is that Metalious *contrives motivation* for the disappearances, while Nabokov erases with the wink of an eye. But why should an effort toward credibility earmark lowbrow fiction? Perhaps because familiar "logic" reassures the lowbrow reader that they're in a comprehensible world. Also because achieving an undetectable craft is more important to the highbrow writer: it's part of what separates the few from the flock.[13] Admittedly, the artlessness of lowbrow writing contributes to its bad name.

But that credibility also disguises, without obliterating, a far starker truth than lowbrow fiction's happy endings foreground. In *Peyton Place* Constance MacKenzie is the only good parent, and she wouldn't have been without tutoring from incredibly wise and incredibly *there* Michael Rossi (ideal high school principal; sexy, unmarried man; coincidentally free mid-year when the previous principal died unexpectedly).

Through the character of Rossi we know that good things don't happen without a great deal of luck. Everything else this little burg has to offer is pretty threatening. Wives cheat on husbands, fathers shirk responsibility, almost everyone marries for self-serving reasons, and the truly good people (Selina, for example) are prey to warped perceptions of the truly wicked (Lucas assaults Selina, he says, because she is "a hot one" who "asks for it").

Contrary to popular assumption that lowbrow fiction sweepingly and irresponsibly erases the chasm between desire and possibility or reality and fantasy, *Peyton Place* acknowledges the breach by splitting characters and by balancing the ill fortune of minor characters with the unlikely good fortune of main characters. One more example is Allison's good friend, Kathy, a perfectly sweet and good young woman. She becomes the victim of Harrington's callous greed when she loses an arm on a carnival ride that he and his son erected with inferior materials. The fact that this plot tidbit is quite expendable underscores its philosophical function.[14]

This substructure throws a shadow over the happy ending and tempers the reconciliation between reality and desire. Tania Modleski affirms that the "submerged plots" of women's popular fiction reveal anger that's not apparent in the obvious plot.[15] Unlike the "apotheosized" Lolita, Selina is left with a murder on her conscience and memories of incest, illegal abortion, her mother's suicide, and a disillusioning romance.

Vindicated or not, Selina faces an unpromising future. And Allison's life cannot finally be regarded as full of promise because it is in effect the *other half* of Selina's.

Though the salient logic of *Peyton Place* rewards "good" characters and disposes of the despicable, there is more hope than promise, more desire than reason in this logic. This fulfillment is as concocted as Humbert's, but probably more appealing to readers who desire a world systematic enough to sustain prophecy and law.[16] It affirms the "congregational"—those who hope that satisfaction of desires will be found by aligning with the community and by repressing impulses that serve the self. It reassures a reader that egregious behavior such as incest, usury, mendacity, and venality result in eviction from the flock and that such separation is undesirable.

The Nabokov reader, on the other hand, may feel that membership in the congregation creates the repression that thwarts individuality and freedom. Yet, as Humbert's fate shows, unrestrained freedom and individuality breed painful consequences.

One program foregrounds the cost of conformity; the other foregrounds the cost of separateness, but neither novel creates a world of pleasure without price. Nor does either book condemn or condone particular behavior. Humbert's relationship with Lolita leads to undesirable consequences similar to those in *Peyton Place*: incarceration, annihilation, separation from the object of desire. Humbert's greatest loss is Lolita herself; his solipsistic fulfillment of desires precludes her right to be. He suffers not because he's a pervert, but for reasons much like Metalious's sufferers: because there is no place where what we desire is what we can have. As a factor *in time*, Humbert must face the fact that he can't recover the potential bliss of childhood; he can only have a bogus reproduction. Constance's recovery of an ideal husband to replace the imperfect non-husband she lost is rendered bogus by the improbability of Michael Rossi's being in Peyton Place. Allison's happy ending is tempered by Selina's unhappy one. All good fortune in Peyton Place is seconded by bad. There is no guarantee; only hope.

Both novels struggle to make sense and comfort of the ways in which the world is likely or not likely to fulfill our basic desires. They give their readers similar ethical interpretations, but surface differences invite different expectations and make different demands on readers. For example, the "night school" prose of *Peyton Place* is likely to exclude no one (except, of course, those who are bored or offended by lack of sophistication and complexity), whereas tone and technique in *Lolita* require that you have learned to recognize verbal jokes and fictive conventions—that you detect the wink. In place of admirable characters, reinforcement for conformist behavior, or hope-inducing plot structures, *Lolita* offers a different *object* for admiration: language itself.

The need for specialized knowledge reinforces the highbrow reader's sense of separation from the flock—one of the ways in which highbrow novels make readers "feel good about themselves." Clearly, Nabokov readers feel clever for being able to detect the allusions, witticisms, and parodical features of the text.[17] Furthermore, the laughter these features evokes creates an aura of immunity and detachment from characters who suffer.[18] To laugh at rich, daring, and attractive Humbert is to know he's not invincible; and his inability to resist temptation brings him down to the level of any reader.

On the other hand, the characters who succeed in *Peyton Place*—

Constance and Allison—have qualities that lowbrow readers can identify with and emulate. Therefore readers can enjoy their rewards for learning to "play by the rules." The stipulation that luck plays a part in success frees the less successful reader from self-condemnation.

Some critics deny that lowbrow fiction provides any self-affirmation, that its readers are at best idling time away[19] or at worst swallowing demeaning propaganda.[20] Though its salient features can be found in genres we've consumed for centuries, popular literature is an easy target. Its plots are formulaic and its characters stereotypes; its language is hackneyed and undetailed; its subject matter seems limited to sex and marriage, crime and punishment, test and triumph; its themes reduce to clichés: "crime doesn't pay"; "love conquers all"; "screw your courage to the sticking point and you shall not fail."

Socially concerned critics are often the most vehement detractors, for they find popular fiction "decidedly biased against females,"[21] "indispensable for pacification,"[22] and "motivated solely by profit."[23] They claim that it "makes no allowance for the female inner self"[24] but "stimulates and allays social anxiety"[25]; that it's nothing but "empty animation [which is] entirely meaningless,"[26] and "an agent in the creation and perpetuation of preexisting sensibility."[27]

Other critics do argue that popular fiction is "useful." Joanna Frye says that novels help women to not be alone with their experience (191). Janice Radway points out that misogynistic novels may be of more help to women than sexually enlightened ones because women have more need to learn how to deal with misogyny.[28] In claiming that evil characters in literature give us a chance to discharge anger, Bruno Bettelheim seems to borrow from Aristotle's defense of emotional literature as a means to purgation and purification.[29] Roland Barthes grants only that popular fiction is productive escapism.[30]

Morris Dickstein says "There's as much that's derivative in high culture, but we judge high by its height, pop by its mean." He believes that we distinguish the types more by size of audience than by formal properties.[31] John Sutherland agrees that "the bestness of bestsellers is not respected."[32]

But none of these supporters seems to look beyond the "what you see is what you get" set of standards to reconsider the literary objects of popular fiction. Since reader response studies began in the sixties, we have learned that we have a very poor notion of what the literary object is, how much it differs from subject to subject, and how much it may vary within one subject under different reading circumstances.

Asking readers themselves to identify what they get out of their reading is also unreliable, for readers, like opinion poll respondents, frequently give the kind of responses they think questioners are looking for or repress responses that they fear would be self-incriminating. Furthermore, work in philosophy, linguistics, and literary criticism throughout the twentieth century has contributed to a general agreement about the "instability of the sign"—the fact that there is no absolute or knowable correlation between the linguistic symbol and its interpretant. Jacques Derrida has labeled this phenomenon the "endless drift of language,"[33] suggesting that reading's effect may be something of endless variety and permutation.

Several years of working with aesthetics philosopher Marcia M. Eaton[34] has also added to my skepticism about absolute values in art. Like the reading object, the function of art is something that defies our attempts to name it.

Yet literary scholars and teachers are pressed into naming benefits, the most common being that novels of genuine sophistication—real art novels—reveal truth, betray cultural contradictions, and counteract the repressive forces of social institutions. We choose to believe that art is life-enhancing, that it impels us toward the beautiful and the true, that it frees us to be healthier people. Aside from accusations from parents and school boards that the artistic programs in schools are frills for which taxpayers should not be assessed, we seldom encounter reasons not to support it.

The question of what kinds of literature deserve to be admired and taught is one of the more important cultural controversies of recent decades.[35] Its class implications have been taken up by Terry Eagleton, who posits that literary studies emerged primarily to enable the elite to distinguish themselves from lower classes, women to study what patriarchs thought they could handle, and the acculturated to prove themselves a distinguished set. He believes that literary opinions are constructed by those who have a stake in keeping their own judgments valorous.[36]

That generally means that literary opinions will be argued on highbrow terms—standards by which popular novels, especially lowbrow novels, are destined to fall short. If we learn to recognize the techniques, structure, and agenda of popular novels, we can evaluate and discuss them on their own terms. If we pay more attention to how lowbrow and middlebrow novels work, how their parts affect the whole, and especially how their happy endings are deconstructed by what precedes, we can provide readers a richer and more accurate assessment of popular literature.

Gans says that the popular readership has had to serve as their own critics because we don't train ourselves in the standards of non-high culture (116-17). Tony Bennett points out that there are plenty of things going on in popular fiction that we just don't recognize because we "don't pay attention to the strategies" (227).

This book explores three major strategies for discovering what's going on in popular fiction: 1) examining the various ways in which each form of the novel works out a reconciliation between what is desired and what is possible—what I refer to in chapter six as "the divided self"; 2) examining how their connections to history and culture determine different *functions* for the three subgenres; 3) examining how the moral and ethical content of each subgenre is influenced by historical, social, and economic conditions. These strategies should enable readers to both determine differences between good and bad lowbrow and middlebrow novels and to apprehend what these novels give to readers other than titillation, escape, or mind massage.

NOTES

1. Some will argue that this is Humbert's book, not Lolita's. But consider: 1) Humbert's tale and his foremost concern are about how he has dismantled the youth of a person he has come to love. Daniel J. Hughes, "Reality and the Hero: *Lolita* and *Henderson the Rain King*," *Modern Fiction Studies 6* (1960-1): 355. Humbert is, as the chapter discusses, Lolita's creator, and through his gaze on this creation directs ours to her as well; 2)Highbrow novels are marked by readers' detachment from main characters, so there is no single protagonist with which the reader strongly identifies.

2. Grace Metalious, *Peyton Place* (1956; New York: Pocket, 1965). All quotations will be cited from this edition.

3. Vladimir Nabokov, *Lolita* (1955; Greenwich, CT: Fawcett, 1958), 254. All further quotations will be cited from this edition.

4. *Morphology of a Folktale* (Austin and London: U of Texas P, 1968). Madonne M. Miner, in *Insatiable Appetites: Twentieth Century Women's Best Sellers* (Westport, CT: 1984), explains that "splitting" personalities among two or more characters, so that a character really represents a salient trait rather than a multi-faceted personality, is a commonplace of folk tales and lowbrow fiction (76).

In *Hamlet and Oedipus*, Ernest Jones describes the process as "decompo-sition" wherein attributes of one individual are disunited and distributed among several characters. (New York, 1955), 149-50. Such distribution explains the stereotyping and exaggeration that are common criticisms of the genres. But *Lolita* uses the same process: see below on the Humbert/Quilty split.

Lolita herself exhibits the opposite trait, which Jones calls "condensation," for, in G.D.Josipovici's terms, she is a "demon disguised as a female child." "*Lolita*: Parody and the Pursuit of Beauty," *Critical Quarterly* (Spring 1964), 39.

5. Here's another instance of metonymic doubling: Roger B. Salomon says Quilty is Humbert's worse half—the "guilty" side. *Desperate Storytelling: Post-Romantic Elaboration of the Mock-Heroic Mode* (Athens and London: U of Georgia P, 1987), 213.

6. Treating Nabokov as a moralist challenges some common critical perspectives (see, for example, Martin Green's assessment of Nabokov's anti-Tolstoian aesthetic in "The Morality of *Lolita*," *Kenyon Review* 28 [1966]). However, Nabokov's moralism is not without its defenders. Alan Pryce-Jones says this book's moral is "You'll pay for your actions." "The Fabulist's Worlds: Vladimir Nabokov," in *The Creative Present: Notes on Contemporary American Fiction*, eds. Nona Balakian and Charles Simmons (Garden City, NY: Doubleday, 1962), 75.

7. The older Harrington provides another good example of "the sins of the father," for he was so determined to have an heir that he kept impregnating his wife, though she suffered miscarriage after miscarriage, until she bore Rodney and died in the process.

8. Anika LeMaire, *Jacques Lacan*, trans. David Macy (London: Rout-ledge and Kegan Paul, 1970), 175.

9. Charlotte represents, according to Green, "the reality amidst the idyll" (373).

10. "The Flaunting of Artifice in Vladimir Nabokov and Jorge Louis Borge," *Wisconsin Studies in Contemporary Literature* 8.2 (1967): 294.

11. Green, 366. According to D.J. Hughes, Humbert's wish content remains the same while he recognizes that attainment of it is self-induced folly (350).

12. Green, 357.

13. Cumbersome contrivance is typical of "discontented salesmen and housewives" taking "night-school classes in creative writing." Otto Friedrich, "Farewell to Peyton Place," *Esquire* (December 1971), 164.

14. Another nearly useless scene in *Peyton Place* fills in one more piece of moral microcosm. Several lushes in town hole themselves up in a basement for six weeks, supplied with gallons of intoxicants. The only damage resulting from this binge is that one of the drunks axes his own foot. Metalious's point seems to be that antisocial behavior can be overlooked if it only hurts the perpetrator.

15. *Loving with a Vengeance: Mass-Produced Fantasies for Women* (Hamden, CT: Archon, 1982), 25 and 58.

16. Frank Kermode, *Sense of an Ending* (1967; New York: Oxford UP, 1977), 14.

17. Barbara Herrnstein Smith maintains that the "culturally dominant

class is gratified by works that are structurally complex and informationally rich—that gratify the exercise of competence." "Contingencies of Value," *Critical Inquiry* 10.1 (September 1983): 29-33.

18. Henri Bergson argues that laughter is incompatible with emotion and that the comic character is dehumanized. *Laughter: An Essay on the Meaning of the Comic*, trans. Cloudesley Brereton and Fred Rothwell (New York: Macmillan, 1928), 87 and 139.

19. Dwight MacDonald suggests that "masscult" provides mere distraction, not even entertainment. *Against the American Grain* (New York: Random, 1962), 4-5.

20. Frederic Jameson says that Puzo's *The Godfather* teaches readers that daily life in America deteriorates because of ethical rather than economic matters and makes us envy the "family" of the Mafia. "Reification and Utopia in Mass Culture," *Social Text* 1 (Winter 1979): 146.

21. Jack Zipes, *Breaking the Magic Spell: Radical Theories of Folk and Fairy Tales* (London: Heinemann, 1979), 136.

22. Umberto Eco, *The Role of the Reader: Explorations in the Semiotics of the Text* (1979; Bloomington: Indiana UP, 1984), 107.

23. Listed by Herbert Gans in *Popular Culture and High Culture: An Analysis and Evaluation of Taste* as one of the four major criticisms of pop fiction. (New York: Basic, 1974), 19.

24. Joanna Frye, *Living Stories, Telling Lives: Women and the Novel in Contemporary Experience* (Ann Arbor: U of Michigan P, 1986), 80.

25. Modleski, 27-8.

26. Georg Lukács, *The Theory of the Novel: A Historico-Political Essay on the Forms of Great Epic Literature* (Cambridge, MA: MIT Press), 93.

27. Clifford Geertz, *The Interpretation of Cultures* (New York: Basic, 1973), 449.

28. *Reading the Romance: Women, Patriarchy and Popular Literature* (Chapel Hill: U of North Carolina P, 1984), 72.

29. *The Uses of Enchantment: The Meaning and Importance of Fairy Tales* (New York: Knopf, 1984), 72. Though he's concerned with the "unthinking pleasures" popular arts enable, Northrop Frye contends that they allow room for the unconventional in a highly conventional society. *The Educated Imagination* (Bloomington: Indiana UP, 1964), 86-91.

30. Barthes says that Verne's *Nautilus* books provide "a dream of cherished isolation." *Mythologies*, trans. Annette Lavers (New York: Hill and Wang, 1972), 53.

31. "Popular Fiction and Critical Values: The Novel as a Challenge to Literary History," *Reconstructing American Literary History*, ed. Sacvani Bercovitch (Cambridge, MA: Harvard UP, 1986), 38 and 60.

32. *Bestsellers: Popular Fiction of the Seventies* (London: Routledge and Kegan Paul, 1981), 3.

33. "Signature, Event, Context," *Glyph I* (1977), 182.

34. See, for example, Eaton's book *Art and Non-Art: Reflections on an Orange Crate and a Moose Call* (Rutherford, NJ: Farleigh Dickinson UP, 1983) and "Where's the Spear?" *British Journal of Aesthetics* 1 (January 1992): 1-12.

35. "Deserves" is an operative word here: Tony Bennett says that our problem is not *value*, but our theory of constructing value. "Marxism and Popular Fiction: Problems and Perspectives," *Southern Review* 15 (July 1982): 219.

36. *Literary Theory* (Minneapolis: U of Minnesota P, 1983), 35-39.

II

QUINTESSENTIAL MIDDLEBROW: THE MAN IN THE GRAY FLANNEL SUIT DOES "THE BEST HE CAN WITH THE WORLD AS HE SEES IT"[1]

Sloan Wilson's novel, *The Man in the Gray Flannel Suit*, for all its past fame and success, is not a very good novel.[2] The plot is contrived, the characters are flat, and their emotions hard to believe. Critic John McNulty rates it "not a very believable book[3]; the *Time* reviewer says it, "Verges on upper-middle class soap opera"[4]; Gerald Weales says "[Tom Rath is] not Everyman, but no man at all."[5]

Other contemporary reviewers found it bogged down in detail. Nora Magid says: "So many extraneous ingredients are tossed [in] . . . it ends up shapeless" with an ending that is "Pollyanna cum Freud."[6] Weales says the book is spoiled by "saccharine clichés," stock characterization, and "a welter of incident as commonplace as it is irrelevant" (525). Several reviewers seemed to be, as I was on the first reading, so absorbed in wondering whether Tom Rath's bold job shift from a family-run endowment firm to The United Broadcasting Corporation would bring him financial ruin that they failed to recognize major themes of the novel.

This chapter argues that many of the complaints about *The Man in the Gray Flannel Suit* derive from applying highbrow standards; others emerge because we're disconnected from the peculiar anxieties of the fifties.[7] For all its faults, Wilson's novel is a wonderful example of a middlebrow novel. The flat characters and cumbersome subplots are apt and essential to its middlebrow intentions. They help to focus readers'

17

attention on the main drama of whether emergent corporate America has the power to eat normal people alive.

Like myth, middlebrow novels address a particular set of anxieties about a changing social order and demonstrate the rewards of conformity to a current standard and the pitfalls of nonconformity. Northrop Frye says that myths persuade us to "adjust."[8] As "parahistory" (Aristotle's definition of myth), the middlebrow novel is a chronicle of people in particular circumstances which values the survival of the state above that of the individual.[9] Mythical stories need a "welter of detail" in order to create the chronicle; they need flat characters so that readers aren't oppressed by the thwarting of individuality. For these features, a mythical novel might easily earn criticism that it "is a rite that insists on the outcome that best serves equilibrium."[10]

Yet as a chronicle of prevailing conditions, myth provides instructions about coping with the external world. Whether its readers know this or not, myth teaches them how to endure. *The Man in the Gray Flannel Suit* is both primer and survival kit.

The mythical protagonist is one who must "fall from innocence" and be initiated into "real life."[11] Since the aim of the initiation is to survive the apprenticeship and accede into the economic order, middlebrow novels may also seem to "bestow legitimacy on the social institution."[12] In other words, they participate in value formation, which is explained by Barbara Herrnstein Smith as the byproduct of mutual modification between our desires and the dynamics of an economic system.[13]

To reiterate, *The Man in the Gray Flannel Suit* is both wonderful as a middlebrow novel and disappointing as a highbrow one because it fulfills these middlebrow conventions:

1. Through contrived subplots and excessive mimetic detail, *The Man in the Gray Flannel Suit* provides a convincingly credible picture of the conditions of economic survival. William H. Whyte, Jr., says that this novel is paradigmatic of corporate life in the American fifties.[14] Louis Coxe writes that: "Without trying to be sociological or symbolical, Mr. Wilson has got more of the late forties and early fifties into his book than any other writer I know...."[15]

2. Its hero is ordinary rather than enviable.

3. The course of events makes clear that the protagonist must give up cherished notions of a "golden age" or a lost Eden where life's responsibilities can be met without sacrificing what

is most desirable. Because what is most desirable (the taboo) is attainable only at great price, the overall tone of a middlebrow novel is conciliatory but cautionary ("Pollyanna cum Freud"): the protagonist who denies his real desire for what's forbidden wins only a consolation prize; protagonists who don't forbear invite retribution.

The compromising protagonist gives another reason that *Man in the Gray Flannel Suit* lacks resonance outside the fifties. Without full understanding of Rath's economic options, it's hard to be pleased by his politically correct choices. He seems pretty dull in contrast to, say, the hero of James Jones's *From Here to Eternity*, whom we can admire for "being his own man." Though Robert E. Lee Prewitt dies for his failure to realign himself with prevailing order, many readers may prefer pugnacity to Pollyanna.

4. A successful outcome for the protagonist is dependent upon a willingness to adapt to changing economic factors.

These conventions also provide certain compensations for readers who are looking for primer and survival kit. Tom's ordinariness provides connection to "ordinary" readers: he turns down the chance to become a big shot so he can be a decent breadwinner and a better-than-decent family man. Contentment with the sidelines is a positive, non-intimidating feature of his portrayal.

On the other hand, ordinariness is not a pervasive rule. Wife Betsy (despite conventional cheeriness about getting up every morning to "fix a good breakfast") is out of the ordinary by being genuinely instrumental in affecting the family fortunes. She's the one who first thinks of parceling Mrs. Rath's land into lots, and she oversees the scheme's realization. She is significant to the partnership without dominating (and probably the prototype of many female real estate agents of our decade). Where Tom is restrained, her freedom to act helps us to "imagine ways" to improve social conditions and to "question and change the limits of change in a conservative society."[16]

The primary balm in middlebrow structure is its implication that the best we can do is pay attention so that nothing worse becomes of us. The fall from grace in this 1950s tale is caused by desires which became less fulfillable in the fifties: for meaningful work, for the freedom to enjoy the moment at hand without concern for "getting ahead," for marriage that is more conjugal than corporate, for the opportunity to redress perceived ill-treatment.

Coxe says that *The Man in the Gray Flannel Suit* is about maintaining and consolidating one's position in the face of "violent disinclination" (157). Both Betsy and Tom are aware of having given over their inclinations. Betsy wonders what has become of the fun they had in their first three months of marriage before the war, yet the suggestive red dress she wears to greet Tom on his return is quickly replaced by housewifely cottons.

When Tom first returned from the war, Betsy declared that the most important thing was for him to work in a job he liked. But as soon as he's made the switch to the broadcasting corporation she scolds him for complaining and encourages him to do whatever the new boss Hopkins wants: "You ought to be thinking it's the best idea in the world!" (110)

Tom's self-conception is dominated by his sense of obligation for his children's future. Though they are only about three, four, and six in the novel, he thinks incessantly about providing college educations for them. Responding to Hopkins' question "What is the most significant fact about you?" Tom replies, "I have children."

Taboos against satisfying the self are the issues of Wilson's subplots, their avoidance being the object of this morality play. Two subplots represent the loss of Eden; one, ironically, involves the war. In contrast to Rath's postwar life fraught with his own lack of desire, passion, and purpose, there was something simple, pure and passionate about his involvement in the war. He had a job to do, orders to follow, and clear goals: destroy the enemy and stay alive; live one day at a time.

The clarity and naturalness provided Tom with what he looks back on as the happiest days of his life. When the war in Europe wound down in 1944, his company of paratroopers was temporarily stationed in Rome awaiting transport to the Pacific front. What was supposed to be a two-day layover turned into forty-nine days, and Tom spent that time living with an eighteen-year-old Italian girl.

Tom is required to check in daily to see if the troops are ready to leave, and each time he finds they are not, he and Maria revel in having each other for one more day. Theirs is the romantic idyll of lowbrow novels—with the cautionary overlay that it must be ephemeral: Tom is already married; his company will be called out at any moment.

One plot contrivance is establishing a reason for Maria to spend this time with a married American soldier who has little money to spend on her. Wilson explains that Maria was hungry for an emotional entanglement because her parents had recently been killed by enemy fire bombs. That she expresses little of the anxiety one might expect from one so recently bereaved and instead engages in the love affair with great delight suggests that she need not be credible to serve her purpose in the novel.

Her enthusiasm also underscores the deliciousness of being able to respond naturally and freely. In general, the war in this novel is an arena where responsive rather than responsible action is required—the direct contrast to corporate America. As a soldier, Tom killed seventeen men, one of them his best buddy. He seems not guilt-ridden, but absolved by his awareness that a soldier kills in order not to be killed.

What precipitated the killing of Hank Mahoney was Rath's sense that as company leader he needed to show new paratroopers how to remain on the offensive after alighting. He had been crawling among his frightened squad, shoving rifles into their hands and thinking, "The Japs had not been afraid to fire—they had taken it as a matter of course that they would kill some of their own men" (94). When he detects a moving figure "out of the corner of his eye," he instantly throws a grenade. Later, when he hears of soldiers looting Japanese corpses for teeth, sabers, even heads to boil for souvenirs, he finds a way to put the incident in perspective:

> The fact that he had been too quick to throw a hand grenade and had killed Mahoney, the fact that some young sailors had wanted skulls for souvenirs, and the fact that a few hundred men had lost their lives to take the island of Karkow—all these facts were simply incomprehensible and had to be forgotten. That, he had decided, was the final truth of the war, and he greeted it with relief, greeted it eagerly. . . . (99)

Being able to act instinctively makes the world of war an emancipation: he does not have to justify each action against a repressive civil norm. "The trick," Tom tells himself here, "is to learn to believe that it's a disconnected world, a lunatic world, where what is true now was not true then. . . " (101). The "sanity" of this paradox, according to Alan Sinfield, is that we recognized by the fifties that we lived in an alienated world, and to deny that, to be made to believe that we're fulfilling some kind of plan, is "a terrible human lie."[17]

Madison Avenue *is* a world which insists on that lie: Tom's only responsibility in his several months at United Broadcasting Corporation is to write a speech for Mr. Hopkins to deliver about the state of mental health care in the country. No one, including Hopkins, knows what the speech is supposed to say or do, though all expect it to have significant impact.

The second lost Eden of *The Man in the Gray Flannel Suit* involves Grandmother Rath, whose incomprehensible world is that of inherited wealth. Her husband's forebears had made a fortune which her older son has lost, but she pretends that that's not happened. She refuses to discuss finances and persists in living in "the style to which she'd grown accustomed." She thinks nothing of asking the grocer himself to leave his till and deliver her a jar of olives.

Her presence in the novel augurs the advent of an age of hard-won wealth, the non-existence of wealth without work. The servant's ability to dupe her and a neurotic son's inability to recognize a wise investment signals the requirements of the new order: guts, drive, vigilance and shrewdness.[18]

Tom's father and the servant, Edward Schultz, are two of the characters in the "morality play" of this novel—caricatures with "humours" ill-suited for success in the world. The elder Rath's humour is nervousness: he handled combat duty no more successfully than he managed the family's assets. Devastated by this ineptitude, he committed suicide.

Schultz's humour stimulates greed, paranoia and jealousy. When Mrs. Rath dies, Tom tells Schultz that he plans to settle some kind of pension on him, after he finds out how much the estate will yield. Schultz retorts: "I don't need your charity! I've probably got a lot more than you have!" (128). He has amassed his savings, a judge discovers, by arranging that several merchants pad Mrs. Rath's bills and split the take with him.

Rath's new boss, Ralph Hopkins, is the caricature of the obsessed businessman. Wilson has given him the frail physique and pumped-up persona of a displaced Wizard of Oz who manages to overcome his failings by sheer main force. He works seven days a week, sixteen hours a day. Nora Magid says Wilson overdoes Hopkins in order to demonstrate the price of success.[19] That price is the loss of his family. He loses a son in combat who might have gone to college if observing his father's ambition had not so dissuaded him, a daughter to an ill-starred marriage, and a wife to loneliness and despair. Like Oz, he is a clever mechanic, force without weight, heat without heart. The only person to remain loyal is his aide-de-camp, Ogden, a Dickensian sycophant.

Caesar Gardella, one of the paratroopers in Rath's company, is the moral inverse of Hopkins. On the one hand, he illustrates the lack of success that comes of uxoriousness. Before the war he was engaged to marry a girl from "back home" in Italy—a cousin of Maria's. After the war he brings his bride to America, and they pursue the American dream in the way a Horatio Alger hero might have.

Working as an elevator operator, he trades shifts whenever his wife (also an elevator operator) does, so that one of them can be home with the children. They send monthly checks to poor relations in Italy. After five years of this they think themselves lucky to be offered a joint caretakership of an apartment building so they don't have to be apart so much.

On the other hand, this same dedication to the family makes Caesar something of the heroic guardian that his name suggests. In telling contrast to Hopkins, Gardella reunites families rather than separates them. When he spots Rath in his gray flannel suit riding the elevator to Hopkins's office, he assumes that Tom is doing all right and approaches him about helping Maria and their son.

Without this intervention Maria would have remained nothing but a sweet memory. Though Tom regarded Maria's pregnancy as a happy occurrence for him—a chance to leave something to posterity should he be killed at Karkow—it never occurred to him to look into her welfare afterwards.

Drawing up plans to send his and Maria's son a hundred dollars a month enables Tom to appease the "lawmakers" of his era as it further distances him from the wartime Eden free of troubling consequences. Wilson takes pains to keep the matter a business deal. A recent picture of Maria shows that she has grown fat and tired and their son is a skinny, intellectual-looking child. Passion is part of memory only; posterity you pay for.

In the post-Edenic business world of this novel, natural inclinations are forever held in check; learning to endure that fact is the hurdle Tom must leap in order to accede into successful corporate life.

Tom fights his own cynicism about the work that he's doing and the people he works for: "Often I feel as though I'd like to kill Ogden. . . . It's strange that I am permitted to kill only strangers and friends" (130). He bristles that his grandmother has "never cooked a meal . . . or washed a diaper, or done a damn thing for herself or anybody else. She's spent at least three million dollars, and her only comment has been that money is boring" (47).

Tom often reminds himself to overrule his passions: "It's absurd to think these things . . . I shouldn't get excited" (168-9). And a daily ration of martinis seems to dull the frustration of never acting upon what outrages him. The peace-attainment ritual of Sunday mornings included martinis in bed, until Betsy and Tom decide that they're going to do "all they must" to "make it." Then the family attends Sunday services. The substitution seems to bear out Ruth Miller Elson's observation that religion as popularized by Billy Graham made it God's duty to enlarge man, rather than vice versa.[20]

Despite the rewards at the ending, this novel is a pretty grim rendering of life in fifties America. Passion, joy, laughter, freedom from care and responsibility, pleasure in work, play of any kind are things of a lost Eden. I was struck by the fact that in 1955 the Rath children never seem to play and are already conditioned to being sent off to watch television to settle them down and give their parents some privacy.

The only recreation Tom and Betsy partake in is a neighborhood cocktail party to celebrate someone's promotion, wherein the primary activity is drinking lots of alcohol. Jonathan Dollimore says that the "normal" state of affairs in the fifties was marked by the abdication of ecstasy and the betrayal of true potential, which wasn't begun to be set right until the sixties when sociologists like R.D.Laing began to critique oppressive family structures.[21] Tom's "fall from innocence" into "real life" means hard work, deferred gratification, and suppression of passions and whims.

What make it bearable, by Wilson's account, are the consolation prize of money and the lesson that the world is not as bad as you might think. Two other guardian angel characters boost Tom's reasons to trust the promises of corporate America. One is Judge Saul Bernstein.[22] He is a man who "detests justice almost as much as he detested violence" (139) because it serves those who can buy it. With an oracle's capacity to read signs and omens and detect hidden truth, Bernstein senses Rath's basic decency and does his own investigating. This uncovers Schultz's scam as well as the size of his and Rath's bank account: $78000 and $9000.

The other is "Buggy" Bugala, an inexperienced independent contractor looking for his chance to make it big—which he sees in the Rath's twenty-acre estate. Unlike our stereotyped nineties contractor, Bugala sizes up his chances for making a deal with the Raths and concludes that "The thing to do [is] . . . try to form some kind of partnership. . . . After all, there was no reason to try to cut Rath out—there would be plenty of profit to go around. . ." (159). Well, give Wilson credit for at least making him inexperienced.

Hopkins is perhaps a third, for like the Wizard of Oz he turns out to be not an ogre, but a man carried away by power who would probably be happy to have acquired friends instead. His efforts to make something of a son of Rath seem to bear this out, as does his too-late efforts to communicate with his daughter and his wife.

Marxists undeniably have fodder here to charge that Rath's life is bearable only because of his improbable luck. Everyday citizens don't stumble upon a judge like Bernstein, a contractor like Bugala, and a boss like Hopkins, who, though obsessed, nevertheless wishes Rath safe passage (and unrancorously finds a "nice" place for him in the company when Rath turns down his offer to be groomed as heir apparent).

The people who make it possible for Tom to become well established and still have more time at home with his wife and kids are not fixtures of the real world but elements of myth, figures which do the work of demonstrating that citizens will be rewarded for observing taboos.

Whether this lack of credibility makes this middlebrow novel an instrument of class containment and a weapon of mass deception or a tool of good counsel for readers who need to learn how to bear unpleasant realities is a difficult question to resolve.

Richard Ohmann says that the essentially upwardly mobile readers of bestsellers learn that "maturity" entails "the acceptance of disturbed social relations."[23] Adorno and Horkheimer would likely argue that because its style requires concentration on the "relentless rush of facts" and because it appeals to the upwardly mobile and not the lower classes, it distracts from real social ills, misses on universality, and only mythifies success.[24]

Jack Zipes would likely argue that because it restricts choices (Rath cannot choose to "demote" his family and be like Gardella, for example), it "fragments consciousness" and only "mimics egalitarianism."[25] Elson contends that much popular literature advocates the "bootstrap theory" and therefore suggests that institutions don't need changing, individuals do.[26]

But the book at least recognizes harsh realities and disturbed social relations. Even Georg Lukács might be called upon in support of the novel's denouement, for it surely fulfills his requirement that the "homecoming" contain irony and not be an unconditional affirmation.[27]

Though the Raths have moved into an aristocrat's home in a posh section of town, though that community will most likely grant the Raths' request for land development rezoning, and though Tom will be making a decent salary at a job that doesn't require him to work overtime, the future is not guaranteed. The job doesn't promise to be more satisfying than the one that entailed thirty rewrites of the same speech;

their wealth will be compromised by child support to Maria's son; educational expenses will keep them slaves of a savings plan for at least a couple decades; and any lapse in vigilance or resolve will tear the fabric of the scheme. Yes, they are wage slaves in the classic Marxian sense, and the book's emphasis on the family's obligation to educate their children is clearly a mechanism which perpetuates that slavery *ad infinitum.*

What is fair to say about *The Man in the Gray Flannel Suit* is that it's a middlebrow myth that denies two other myths: the personal myth that "you can have it all," as well as the Marxian myth that the ruling class will take it all from you. In the words of the *Time* reviewer, the novel teaches Tom that "he is not Faust, nor the corporation Mephistopheles" (102). The presence of contrasting characters and contrasting worlds has the "discursive capacity" to create the dialogue that Altieri is looking for "between empirical conditions and underlying principles."[28] "Literature . . . if it asserts anything," according to Leslie Fiedler, asserts "the . . . ambiguity of all moral imperatives."[29]

Do most readers note the ambiguity, or is the dialogue neutralized by incredible characters and plot contrivances? The answers are equivocal, I think, because our detached perspective and our greater familiarity with situations like Tom Rath's make it easier for nineties readers to notice what is improbable.

But credibility itself is of little concern in a mythical story where events must work out according to a social paradigm rather than a rational or empirical one: the appearance of reality not reality itself entices readers to the reading. Plot elements and characters must be paradigmatic rather than unique in order to carry the burden of a moral story. Jane Tompkins says that stereotypes are integers in social equations that teach what to emulate or shun; being widely shared is what confers popularity and acceptability on characteristics of novels.[30]

The central character needs to be individualized only in aspects that cause the clash with the social order: in Tom's case it is necessary only that he be anxious and frustrated, yet lacking in that requisite "desire" to be a successful executive, that he have in his background those lost Edens of unfettered love and unearned wealth, that he have a worthy wife and nice children who desire and "deserve" his financial commitment.

Most importantly for a happily ending middlebrow novel, he must come equipped with the abundance of self-discipline which enables him to meet the demands of a rationalist society.[31] With more talent, more imagination, less responsibility, more carelessness, a stronger ego, Tom would not serve the purpose of demonstrating how the typical man will fare by being typical. That Tom's fate clearly represents a kind of "law of averages" makes it impossible that readers can completely ignore the ambivalences of this myth.

Now whether *The Man in the Gray Flannel Suit* does this *well* is another question. Do novels have to appear as contrived and dully crafted as this in order to succeed as middlebrow novels? The answer is clearly no. Earl Foell's praise notwithstanding, Wilson is just not a very good writer.[32] Better middlebrow novels, such as *From Here to Eternity* and *Catcher in the Rye*, remain readable and stimulating beyond their year of publication, because of greater credibility and more engaging characters. But a novel like *The Man in the Gray Flannel Suit* serves a purpose for a time.

NOTES

1. Sloan Wilson, *The Man in the Gray Flannel Suit* (1955; New York: Pocket, 1956), 194. Also serialized in *Collier's*, June-July, 1955.) All further quotations will be cited from the Pocket edition.

2. It did get a couple of raves. Earl W. Foell in the *Christian Science Monitor* said "Sloan Wilson is an expert writer. . . . If his novel cannot be called major with a capital letter, it is because its subject matter does not cover universal experience." "Travails and Travels of a Commuter," 21 July 1955, sec. 2: 11. *Collier's* advertised that this Literary Guild feature would be well received by their readers as a serialized novel. Whyte quotes an ad billing the novel as "One of the rare books of recent vintage leaving one with a feeling of pride to be a member of the human race" (279).

3. *NY Times*, 17 July 1955, 18.

4. "Slipped Disk," 18 July 1955, 102.

5. "Life in Modern America," *Commonweal* (26 August 1955): 526.

6. *New Republic*, 8 August 1955, 20. Rose Feld of the *New York Herald Tribune* says *The Man in the Gray Flannel Suit* is "a thoughtful, searching novel," but the characters "lack reality." "Stepping out of the Army Uniform into that of the Junior Executive," 17 July 1955, sec. 6: 1.

7. The appendix summarizes what those anxieties are and the conditions that produced them.

8. *The Educated Imagination* (Bloomington: Indiana UP, 1964), 140.

9. K.K. Ruthven, *Myth, The Critical Idiom*, 31, ed. John D. Jump (London: Methuen, 1976), 8-10. Bronislaw Malinowski makes a similar point:

that myth supports general rather than individual needs and subjugates individuality to the importance of being part of a race. *Sex, Culture, and Myth* (London: Hart-Davis, 1963), 301-2.

10. Lévi-Strauss, *The Savage Mind* (London: Weidenfeld and Nicholson, 1966), 30. Roland Barthes says that myths "preserve the status quo." *Mythologies*, trans. Annette Lavers (New York: Hill and Wang, 1972), 155.

11. Daniel G. Hoffman, *Form and Fable in American Fiction* (New York: Oxford UP), 10. Lemaire identifies fall from innocence as the "fundamental separation" (of the unified self, which the infant perceives in its natal bond with the mother); myth pretends to restore the bond by representing the moment of separation in the story and providing a mythical solution.

12. Jean-François Lyotard, *The Post-Modern Condition: A Report on Knowledge*, trans. Geoff Bennington and Brian Massumi (1979; Minneapolis: U of Minnesota P, 1984), 39.

13. "Contingency of Value," *Critical Inquiry* 10.1 (1983): 15, 17.

14. *The Organization Man* (Garden City, NY: Doubleday, 1956), 146, 278.

15. 14. *Yale Review*, "Recent Fiction," 45 (1955): 157. In the *Saturday Review*, James Kelly called the book "comfortable" and "enlightening," with a "Leica-like focus." 23 July 1955, 9.

16. Frye, 150-1.

17. *Society and Literature, 1945-1970: The Context of English Literature* (New York: Holmes E. Meier, 1983), 77.

18. Elson says that the Depression changed the key ingredient of success from virtue (a la Horatio Alger) to desire (319).

19. The *Time* reviewer says he "remains a blueprint" (102).

20. *Myths and Mores in American Best Sellers* (New York and London: Garland, 1985), 188.

21. "The Challenge of Sexuality" (in Sinfield), 54.

22. It's interesting that in this post-war novel the crook has a German name—Schultz—and the wisest, most sensitive and fair-minded character a Jewish one.

23. Ohmann says that bestsellers teach that "to be unhappy was your own fault in a prosperous America. . . ." "The Shaping of the Canon: U.S. Fiction 1960-1975," *Critical Inquiry* 10.1 (1983). 201, 212.

24. Theodor W. Adorno and Max Horkheimer, "The Culture Industry: Enlightenment or Mass Deception," in *Dialectic of the Enlightenment*, trans. John Cumming (New York: Continuum, 1986), 127, 135.

25. *Breaking the Magic Spell: Radical Theories of Folk and Fairy Tales* (London: Heinemann, 1979), 102. Elsewhere Zipes acknowledges that myth has the potential to bring about good effects, for it "expresses the need for greater justice, opposes socio-political repression" (39).

26. 73. Wilson's novel seems to support Elson's charge, when, for example, Tom's cynicism blocks his ease of entry into corporate echelons.

27. *The Theory of the Novel*, trans. Anna Bostock (Cambridge, MA: MIT Press, 1971), 135-145.

28. Charles Altieri, "An Idea and Ideal of a Literary Canon," *Critical Inquiry* 10.1 (1983): 46, 54.

29. *What Was Literature?: Class Culture and Mass Society* (New York: Simon and Schuster, 1982), 129.

30. *Sensational Designs: The Cultural Work of American Fiction 1790-1860* (New York: Oxford UP), xvi-xvii.

31. Naomi Scheman, *Engenderings: Constructions of Knowledge, Authority, and Privilege* (New York: Routledge, 1993), 86.

32. The weakness is perhaps more readily seen by a later book of his, *A Summer Place*, which was appropriately made into a slick Hollywood movie about mismated lovers at last reuniting.

III

THE NOVEL AND ITS READERSHIP—
FROM DESCARTES
TO THE MAUVE DECADE

The novel is a genre spawned by two features of the Age of Reason.[1] One is empiricism, which disrupted the "community of believers" by repealing the church's and the state's right to proclaim what was true. Truth became a matter of direct observation; anyone with eyes and ears could draw their own conclusions. The second feature is capitalism; the demise of feudalism liberated every individual from a fixed position in society. Readers needed different stories to help them live in this new world.

Under these influences the novel evolved from earlier narrative forms of the epic and the romance. Both the earlier genres cast the individual in a subordinate relationship to god and society. The epic is concerned with the fate of nations rather than individuals; only individuals of heroic stature, those favored by the gods, had the potential to appease the heavens and affect the general welfare.[2] The capacity of epic protagonists to surpass human limitations and do the will of the gods confirmed their worth and restored order to the state.

The romance implies that any individual can *make* themselves worthy by appeasing the gods of the hamlet, by acknowledging subjugation to god and the crown, and by sacrificing the self for the sake of the community. Fealty to a national or spiritual cause (for males) or the formation of a sanctioned sexual union (for either males or females) creates a social harmony where selfhood is insignificant or even undesirable.

The novel casts individuals into a more volatile relationship to society. As the church and state exert less suasion, the arena of control over an individual's destiny and the place where formative precepts are laid down becomes the home. With their realm of support thus shrunken, novel protagonists must work to appease the gods of the hamlet and the heavens as well as the gods of the haberdashery.

Position outside the home is theirs to determine. Capitalism requires that individuals *do* something with their lives, and its attendant Protestant theology teaches that whoever passively accepts the given lot in life is guilty of unfaithful husbanding of this birthright. Ian Watt says the novel springs from a society that values "becoming" rather than being, where individual responsibility is the norm (60, 31).

Thus compelled to venture away from the natal niche, yet tethered to the "will of the father,"[3] every novel's protagonist is challenged to find the "middle way." Such is the dilemma of "the Cartesian subject," whom Naomi Scheman describes as a revolutionary individual: "the bearer of modern epistemic authority [and bourgeois] . . . rights; the self-made capitalist, the citizen of the nation state, and the Protestant bound by conscience and a personal relationship to God."[4]

I see the three subgenres of novels I'm working with in this book as dealing in different ways with this dilemma. In lowbrow fiction the tension between self-determination and security is resolved when the character finds identity *in* the natal niche; that is, the protagonist discovers an independent self by choosing the spot in the scheme of things that has been hers to assume all along.

But in true romance fashion, she must leave home to find home, for the will of the father is not tested under the father's roof; she cannot *choose* an identity that has been hers all along. Instead of yielding to the desire for safety or the temptation of immediate pleasure, lowbrow protagonists must *risk* doing *what they've already been told is right to do* in order to achieve a satisfactory place in life.

Like a typical fairy tale as it is analyzed by Bruno Bettelheim,[5] the lowbrow novel gives a psychological account of achieving adulthood that requires giving up the easy security of parental protection. But the novel differs from the fairy tale by providing access to the inner life of the protagonist[6] and by recasting antagonists and assistants as real world events and people.

The wolf in "Little Red Riding Hood" becomes Lucas Cross in *Peyton Place*; the brave woodsman becomes Michael Rossi. The safety that Allison must give up is denial of sexuality. Early in the novel, when Allison had window-peeped at Lucas raping Selina, she repressed this experience and thereafter curtailed her friendship with Selina. Forgoing the "safety" that such repression affords, she later reclaims her *home* in Peyton Place by returning to support Selina's acquittal when she is tried for Lucas's murder.

Her mother must also learn to see sexuality as worth the risk and accept that both she and her daughter can be fulfilled rather than exploited through sexuality. Both must learn to trust that there are more Michael Rossis than Lucas Crosses in the world, and that they have the power to distinguish between the two types. Through taking a better look at the world, both women earn the right to reside in Peyton Place without anxiety. The lowbrow admonition to accept "what you are by nature" is reinforced by the fact that both Constance's and Allison's "true loves" come *from* the city *to* Peyton Place (as the Prince comes to Cinderella's humble cottage).

Because many critics are antagonized by the lowbrow plot implication that "woman's nature" is to seek nothing more than sexual fulfillment, it's important to notice that what female protagonists do in essence is *take a risk* (give up the safety of "home") that promises to free them from dependency or a position of tactical retreat.

Perhaps until the sexual liberation of the sixties, sexuality could serve as a universal marker of woman's power, will, and ascension into selfhood. Now that women have other means at hand to show strength of will and independence (the wife in Grisham's *The Firm*, for example, is a woman who saves her own self-esteem and her husband's life by being brave, clever, quick, and independent) sexuality loses its flexibility as a symbol.

I make this point to suggest that in terms of what these novels do, their static contents are less significant than their dynamic effects. A brief look back at examples of low, middle and highbrow novels from the era of the novel's birth suggests that each of these subgenres must use the materials and mindset of the society they spring from. The simultaneous existence of highbrow, middlebrow, and lowbrow also suggests that the subgenres are *not* by-products of social stratification or a reading public abased by mass education.[7]

In one of the earliest examples of lowbrow novels, Richardson's heroine Pamela[8] achieves strength and independence solely by controlling her sexuality. Pamela's is a more clear-cut power struggle than the MacKenzie women's. She, too, tests the strength of her parents' teachings by going to a place where she can neither depend on them to protect her nor escape Mr. B's attentions. Pamela must learn to handle him, yield to his advances and thereby ruin herself, or flee. In short, she must derive strength and self-determination from the training of her natal niche; if she succumbs, she loses personhood, power, and property.

In the more contemporary novel, the social order is a more flexible moral arena where Constance can learn by trial and error. Having a sexual relationship with Allison's father does *not* ruin her, but it leaves her in the humiliating position of trying to live a lie. Running her own business without a man's support helps her to gain self-confidence. But what confirms her personhood is a mutually satisfying relationship with Michael Rossi.

The highbrow novel is an inverse of this pattern, for here the protagonist perceives that adherence to the social order obliterates identity and self-esteem. For Humbert to deny that his love for Annabelle Leigh was real or to accept Charlotte Haze as an adequate compensation is to join the ranks of the "dull, sedate and reliable."[9] Thus he is obliged, as all highbrow heroes are, to commit an egregious act in order to distance himself from the mass of humanity. Conformity is self-annihilation. Better to risk exile or exclusion than to be nothing—as the rogue in Richardson's second novel, *Clarissa*, suggests: "If I give up my contrivances, I shall be but a common man."[10]

Clarissa becomes a highbrow novel by virtue of the protagonist's attitude toward the will of the father. Where Pamela transcends her social position by adhering to parental wisdom, Clarissa refuses to honor her father's behest that she marry the boorish Roger Solmes. Running away with Lovelace without benefit of marriage is not exactly criminal but certainly ruinous behavior for an eighteenth-century virgin.

Her independence yields nothing but misfortune. Like Humbert, she cannot surmount the social order, but also like Humbert she never really regrets that she did not obey her father. She would rather have been misbed by Lovelace than by Solmes. Though she cannot endure the world of her own making, neither can she endure one *not* of her making.

In their concerns with finding themselves by coming to terms with the will of the *father* or by conforming to existing social order, highbrow and lowbrow protagonists evolve from their romance counterparts. Both seek self-determination. More like an epic hero, the middlebrow protagonist begins as a determined self and struggles to perform the will of the *gods* without losing that self in the process.

That means that middlebrow protagonists are less preoccupied about finding meaningful personal relationships. In adult middlebrow novels the main characters are usually already married; in youthful middlebrow, they're pre-adolescent or otherwise immunized from romantic preoccupations (by being students at unisex schools, for example).

Because they're more or less established in a home place, they test the waters or challenge the boundaries of that place to see how far they can take self-serving or self-aggrandizing behavior before it has expulsive effects. When the tether is stretched too far, they must learn to readjust (or pay the price for failure to readjust) their wishes with respect to what is offered by the world beyond their natal niche. Defoe's Moll Flanders, though something of a caricature, typifies middlebrow behavior in always "keeping her eye on the main chance," reevaluating, and revising her behavior when it leads her into trouble.

It seems true that in the contemporary era highbrow novels are written for a limited (highly educated) reading public who want to establish a social distance from other societal groups. It also seems true that a lot of "pulp fiction" written in the last hundred or so years (I'm thinking of Horatio Alger for starters) is written explicitly for a readership consciously struggling upward (who now perhaps buy the "self-help" books that promise different ways of winning in the world).

For most of the eighteenth and the beginning of the nineteenth century, bourgeois or middlebrow literature such as the novel, the newspaper, and periodicals seemed able to coexist more peaceably with aristocratic and folk literature—perhaps only because readers had less to choose from. During a good part of the eighteenth century novels were so few in number that novel readers read all of them[11] and judged them not so much by artistry, but according to how well they represented the human character,[12] satisfied a conventional moral scheme,[13] or entertained readers.[14] Though the church was becoming marginalized in the eighteenth century, its capacity to influence a "conventional moral scheme" was stronger than it is today.

Pamela was a huge success from the moment of its publication, when its readership included both aristocracy and a goodly number of servants.[15] Richardson is extremely skillful in straddling a line that would exclude no social classes.

The leisured/monied readers who might have been outraged at this tale of a servant rising above her station found a good deal to like in this book. Upper-class readers might have felt superior because of Pamela's social status, but all readers gain amusement or suspense from knowing more than Pamela does about Mr. B's designs. Mr. B.'s ignorance of Pamela's inner life gives all readers an edge on him. The story has universally appealing qualities of suspense and titillation (Will Pamela succumb? Will Mr. B ravish her?), while the genre itself provides the pleasure of eavesdropping on someone's private life.

Ian Watt suggests that this voyeuristic quality of the novel was a welcome solace for the privatization of life begun by the end of the feudal era (185-87). Enhanced by Richardson's realistic medium of "letter writing," the accumulation of intimate and real-seeming details of a person's life provides the reader with the heady opportunity to sit in judgment over characters somehow inferior to themselves. William Hazlitt said that reading *Pamela* was like "reading evidence in a Court of Justice."[16]

While the break-up of the feudalism promised more comfortable, self-fulfilling lives to the lower social orders, it also deprived them of the conciliations of stable social order. All social classes, in fact, might have been inclined to worry about stability—who do you trust, who do you stick by, where's home when you move out of the old neighborhood? Not only does *Pamela* suggest to readers from the lower classes that a break-up of the old system has great promise, it also suggests to upper orders that life won't be so different after all.

Watt notes that Richardson extends his novel two hundred pages past the usual matrimonial ending to display how Pamela fares in her elevated station. The scenario assures readers that Pamela is no ill-bred upstart, but a gracious young woman capable of accepting her good fortune with composure and restraint.[17] For upper classes, it assuages fears of usurpage; for lower classes, fears of inadequacy.

Pamela provides assurance that changes in the social order can be survived by learning how to respond to them. It also reinforces common wisdom: prudence is rewarded, but giving in to momentary whims endangers long-range well-being. Yet the message is not a sop, for it requires that the readership accept a new measure of a person's worth—no longer blood, but character, self-restraint, and morality.[18]

In designing a novel to convey such a message, Richardson aims at a particular audience with particular sorts of naiveté, anxiety, morality, and class consciousness.[19] Clearly, some features of this novel are designed to address the social conditions of the time and place of the writing.

The novels I'm writing about were written by Americans in the nineteen-fifties, and I intend to show throughout the text how particular social conditions of the fifties determine unique themes and issues of the high, middle, and lowbrow fiction of that era. But I also want to emphasize that lowbrow, middlebrow, and highbrow fictions exist because they address the differing needs of readerships that coexist in any time period.

The above discussion implies that authors were less consciously producing highbrow, middlebrow and lowbrow novels when the novel first evolved. It seems likely that such consciousness took hold in America in the middle of the nineteenth century.

Nina Baym says that the 1840s and 50s were a "golden moment" in American reading, for a great variety of novels were read by a wide variety of readers (60). Reviewers in mid-century regarded "interesting" as high praise and felt that readers "if left to themselves . . . will not go far astray."[20]

That easy consensus was fostered in part by a still god-fearing society and by, says Baym, a Social Darwinistic tenet that human beings in the natural process of improvement will select what assists that improvement (45-46). Around this time, however, the "good read" became suspect as frivolous, and "enchaining interest" hinted at concern over our "diseased love of undue excitement" (32).

We began to fear that "if left to themselves" the public would wallow in affairs of the flesh and forget anything high-minded. It also seems that as long as a catholic sense of morality supports general public opinion, that public is freer to indulge varieties of opinions. Conversely, the more that a universal sense of goodness and truth fades, the more anxious we become about finding a structural framework to buttress a sagging sense of human dignity.

Lawrence Levine reports that in the same time frame, "culture" came to mean refinement rather than entertainment.[21] Levine's book details how performance arts evolved in the nineteenth century into separate highbrow and lowbrow forms;[22] in the last third of the century, opera and orchestra conductors and theater directors, for example, strove for authenticity and reproductive purity rather than for enthusiastic audiences. Scheman says that the construction of the Cartesian subject is marked by the "centrality of discipline" (88); the "privileged" are those "who have conquered the sexual, dependent, mortal, and messy parts of themselves. . . ." The ability to *restrain* oneself became a mark of the worthy person.[23] Self-worth equaled self-control.

At the beginning of the century, traveling theater and music companies performed Shakespeare and grand opera in far-flung cities to heterogeneous audiences given free rein to express their approval and criticism throughout performances. The featured play or opera was frequently edited into a form likely to draw the most approval and the least criticism; action was heightened, recitative cut, and crowd-pleasing (and usually irrelevant) olios inserted, for example.[24]

By the end of the century the natural responsiveness of audiences was regarded as a great intrusion on the efficacy of a performance, and tampering with an artist's work as written was regarded as sacrilege. "Sacralization" is in fact the term Levine uses to describe what happened to art forms at the turn of the century (240). He illustrates its aptness with views such as Henry James's: "The office of Art is second only to that of religion" (150).

The corresponding literary move was engineered by "serious" novelists of the last half of the decade—Melville, George Eliot, Henry James, and Flaubert—who also worked to purify the company they'd keep by removing the genre from capitalism and commerce.[25] Baym says that the "didacts'" efforts to raise the novel above its basis in pleasure split the novel into the popular and elite forms that we know today and that Eliot was on the "ground floor of dividing popular from academic" novels by insisting on seriousness (40-42).

Tompkins, Lovell and Douglas contend that a gendered power struggle in nineteenth-century America reduced tolerance for bourgeois and folk art forms and aggravated the tendency to discredit novel reading.[26] In something of a power vacuum created by the deterioration of a catholic morality, women novelists of the era suggested that the sensitivity and compassion of women and children, rather than the directives of God or men, would provide the transforming power for social ills.[27]

Overall, the increasingly sanctimonious respect for "highbrow" art which began in the late nineteenth century seems motivated less by snobbery than by fear that we were losing the exalted capacity of self-control. The discipline required by highbrow reading seems to have become a replacement for the discipline required by a universal social order. Perhaps a similar fear triggers our desire to hang onto a literary canon that excludes self-indulgent works and in our concern over quota hiring in academic institutions. Dinesh D'Souza views with some alarm the replacement of Western Great Books by third-world literatures and the practice of establishing minority hiring quotas in American higher education:

> If the university model is replicated in society at large, far from bringing ethnic harmony, it will reproduce and magnify in the broader culture the lurid bigotry, intolerance, and balkanization of campus life.[28]

We must assume that D'Souza is not denigrating minority cultures, but arguing that letting go of high culture standards means letting go of much more that we hold dear, including a cherished ideal of developing a superior society by nurturing superior individuals and suppressing natural desires and impulses.

Gedin believes that the book market of the Western world is becoming that of a mass society, with completely different cultural patterns from those of the nineteenth century, and that the novel, as the product of a bourgeois society, is a prime indicator of that move (9-10). His analysis suggests that what we fear (and, paradoxically, this seems to be D'Souza's fear) is homogeneity.

That fear is augmented by our American mindset, which says that uniformity is mediocrity. Our modern, Cartesian bent of mind includes beliefs that we can evade commodification and mechanization, that effort makes us "better," and that our minds can control impulses toward passion, sex, and violence. Yet, want to or not, we are being pulled in the opposite direction by a "culture industry" dominated by MTV, rock music, and an insistence on bodily awareness.

The raw physicality of our current popular media and the perception of increased violence and rampant sexuality in our neighborhoods convince us that we are in decline. Yet at the same time we are increasingly anti-Cartesian in our anti-intellectualism and our politically correct egalitarianism. The fifties foreshadowed a fear of elitism in their rejection of "egghead" individuals like Adlai Stevenson. The sixties projected us into an era of physical liberation that we both want and fear.

One thing we can do to help ourselves understand how culture may address these concerns, it seems to me, is to stop assuming that "high art" serves high ends and "low art" brings us low. Since we've lost faith in Social Darwinism, we look to art and academia to carry the burden of social amelioration. As a consequence, we've put all our trust in the novel form which we think best serves that end and learned to look with alarm at what seems to pull us in the opposite direction.

But these assumptions are ill-grounded in what we know about what various art forms actually do. I believe there is at least one important reason to treasure lowbrow culture and one important reason to be leery of highbrow culture in terms of their contributions to a healthier society. But we must learn to discern the real function of popular art forms if we are to teach and use them to our best advantage.

NOTES

1. See Tom Conley in a foreword to Louis Marin's *Portrait of the King*, trans. Martha M. Houle, *Theory and History of Literature*, 57 (Minneapolis: U of Minnesota P, 1988), vi-xvii; Per Gedin, *Literature in the Marketplace*, trans. George Bisset (Woodstock, NY: Overlook, 1977), 144; K. K. Ruthven, *Myth* (London: Methuen, 1976), 48; Jane Tompkins, *Sensational Designs: The Cultural Work of American Fiction 1790-1860* (New York: Oxford UP, 1985), 26; Ian Watt, *The Rise of the Novel: Studies in Defoe, Richardson and Fielding* (Berkeley: U of California P, 1964), 10-13; Jack David Zipes, *Breaking the Magic Spell: Radical Theories of Folk and Fairy Tales* (London: Heinemann, 1979), 58.

2. Those of "exemplary subjectivity" in Lukács's term. *The Theory of the Novel*, trans. Anna Bostock (Cambridge, MA: MIT Press, 1971), 137.

3. I use the term because it fits the patriarchal sensibility that dominates the novel's lifespan.

4. "Though This Be Method, Yet There Is Madness in It: Paranoia and Liberal Epistemology," *Engenderings: Constructions of Knowledge, Authority, and Privilege* (New York: Routledge, 1993), 85.

5. *Uses of Enchantment: The Meaning and Importance of Fairy Tales* (1975; New York: Knopf, 1977), 76.

6. Watt, 205. See also Vladimir Propp, *Theory and History of Folklore*, Theory and History of Literature, 5, ed. Anatoly Lieberman, trans. Ariadna Y. Martin, et al. (Minneapolis: U of Minnesota P, 1984).

7. Dwight MacDonald asserts that " 'trash' came into being when more people learned to read." *Against the American Grain* (1952 New York: Random, 1962), 18. It would follow that what is written for lower classes is lower in worth.

8. Many critical appraisals argue that Pamela's artful duplicity adds a measure of irony that prevents the novel from fitting into my lowbrow category. See, for example, Paul Parnell, "The Sentimental Mask," *PMLA* 78 (1963): 529-35. Nevertheless, *Pamela can* be read as a lowbrow novel (and probably was read as a lowbrow novel), and, since it is more well known than other examples from that era, I will use it as such for purposes of illustration

9. Vladimir Nabokov, *Lolita* (1955; Greenwich, CT: Fawcett, 1958), 242.

10. Samuel Richardson, *Clarissa*, Everyman's Library (1747; London: Dent, 1932), III, 208.

11. 44. Gedin's statistics are from English publishers among whom seven novels were published in 1700, 40 in 1780.

12. Watt, 13.

13. Gedin says that novels were rated primarily on their morality and that middle-class readers before 1850 exhibited remarkably similar tastes (17). Nina Baym reports that "didactic" expressed approbation for a serious novel. *Novels, Readers, and Reviewers: Responses to Fiction in Antebellum America* (Ithaca: Cornell UP, 1984), 28.

14. Baym, 55.

15. Gedin says that Pamela was a "culture heroine" to a "powerful sisterhood" of serving girls (17).

16. Watt, 34.

17. Zipes would probably discredit *Pamela* for its failure to "manufacture discontent" sufficient for the motivation of action, but the novel does suit his concept of "revolutionary" folk art in that its common heroine develops talents to pursue changes in social relations (3, 51, 34), as does Elizabeth Bennett a century later.

18. Gedin, 13 and 144.

19. Ruth Miller Elson's, *Myths and Mores in American Best Sellers* (New York and London: Garland, 1985), is an interesting study of how our concept of "other" attaches itself to different groups as economic and social factors change. Americans have a history of scapegoating first one ethnic group and then another, usually the most recently arrived immigrants, but always those who compete for jobs—blacks, Hispanics, women, and homosexuals in our era.

20. Terry Lovell, *Consuming Fictions* (London: Verso, 1987), 214.

21. *Highbrow/Lowbrow: The Emergence of Cultural Hierarchy in America* (Cambridge, MA: Harvard UP, 1988), 56-57.

22. Besides Levine's, other interesting studies of how Victorian ideologies intersected with the arts and academia in the nineteenth century are Baym's, Gedin's, Zipe's, Tompkins's, Ann Douglas's, *The Feminization of American Culture* (New York: Knopf, 1977), and the first two chapters of Terry Eagleton's *Literary Theory* (Minneapolis: U of Minnesota P, 1983).

23. 85-88. In *The Greening of America* Charles Reich discusses how American schools before the present era aimed not to educate, but to program bodies to adapt better to factory hours (New York: Random), 31-33.

24. Levine, 72-76 and 221-22.

25. And, according to Terry Lovell, to thereby turn it for the first time into "literature" (29).

26. Zipes, 12 and 59.

27. See Tompkins, 123-28, and Douglas, 77.

28. Dinesh D'Souza, "Illiberal Education," *Atlantic* (March 1991), 79.

IV

THE SHAPE OF THE BROWS

In chapter three I argue that the novel emerged as a genre when the social functions of earlier narrative forms were no longer appropriate for a reading public liberated from a fixed position in society and compelled into the competitive world of capitalism. Here I will argue that because "form follows function," textual and structural features come together on a predictable basis to earmark highbrow, middlebrow, and lowbrow forms as they depict variant schemes for coping with changing social conditions.

Lowbrow novels, often called "formula fiction,"[1] are as easy to recognize as they are to criticize. They feature flat characters, plain language, and predictable plots which begin with an action or agent that threatens the status quo of the protagonist. The hero is put to a test which she'll survive only if she recognizes and accepts assistance from an agent of good; if the hero passes the test, the ending is not simply a renewal of the threatened status but elevation to higher status.

Narrative techniques are straightforward to avoid the ironic potential of multiple viewpoints. "Meanwhile back at the ranch" scenes are used to keep readers apprised of the strength of enemy forces and to indicate prevailing moral order, but they're not used, as they are in middlebrow fiction, to critique protagonists' behavior.[2]

Lowbrow protagonists must be easy to identify with so that the test can become the reader's: in effect readers step into the heroes' trials and become emotionally committed to their success. Readers expect that there will be a reward for toughing it out. Their sense of "failure by association" is indicated in the refusal by Radway's readers to read books that don't turn out favorably (71, 156).

43

There are lowbrow protagonists who fail. *Forever Amber*[3] provides a classic example of and explanation for the unhappy ending. In the final chapter, Amber makes a fool of herself by trusting a false report that her lover, the father of her children, is waiting for her in Calais. She rushes to meet him there, not knowing that she'll find him vacationing with his wife. The wife can be regarded as Amber's alter ego—the demurring, unassertive *lady* that Amber could have been if she hadn't tried to win a man by being a temptress. Though Winsor's novel is unusual in making the rival the protagonist, Margaret Ann Jensen says that romances often feature a rival man or woman who "teaches us what not to be."[4]

The opening scene of *Forever Amber*, which never ties in with the rest of the novel, reveals that Amber's nobleman father was killed in battle, that her mother died in childbirth, and that she was then cared for by poor relations. The scenario counsels that Amber's life as a conniving courtesan is not her true destiny; if she had waited for her pedigree to become known, *she* could have had this desirable husband waiting for her in Calais. *Forever Amber* is an all-time bestseller;[5] its success indicates that readers accept this uncomfortable ending because the novel's larger implication is that women are "born to the purple" and sell themselves short by thinking their only allure is sex.

In order for readers to identify strongly with protagonists, lowbrow fiction requires prose of low resolution: Nothing from characters' appearance to their clothing, careers, consumer habits, and social lives to locales, settings, and domiciles is presented with enough precision to disenfranchise any reader. Cawelti says that formula fiction takes the reader "out of himself to confirm an idealized self-image." Heroes may be better or luckier than ourselves, but there must be nothing in the story that threatens our ability to share the triumphs or reprieves (18-19). Meant to be "typical," protagonists are usually vaguely described in order to avoid naming characteristics clearly dissonant with their readers'. E.H.Gombrich says in *Art and Illusion* that "lack of elaboration guarantees the absence of contradictory clues."[6]

When foreign or historically remote settings are used, what is not familiar, ordinary, or stereotypical is broadly sketched so that "otherness" becomes easily known and thereby "de-othered." The "accent is on the familiar rather than the exotic."[7] Richard Nelson, an ancient historian who reviewed Colleen McCullough's, *The First Man in Rome*, pointed out that much of McCullough's history and archaeology were accurate, but of the period of Rome most known in stereotyped notions of "ancient Rome"—two centuries after the setting of McCullough's novel.[8] Leon Uris says "all it takes is a crash course" to write the kind of historical fiction he does.[9]

The popularity of the film *Dances with Wolves* seems to bear out the powerful appeal of making the "other" more like ourselves. Helping us to accept outsiders as more like us than we thought is part of the positive cultural work that lowbrow art does. Recognizing the importance of "making the strange familiar" should give us reason to judge popular writing by a different rubric than the literary/poetic standards we apply to highbrow writing.

Lowbrow language is also suited to eliciting a uniform response from readers. Sentence structure and vocabulary are prosaic, and figurative language is either absent or clichéd. Standardized, almost formularized descriptions and clipped and stilted dialogue create a kind of "transparent medium" of high accessibility and high predictability through which the reader can make an unimpeded "escape" into the subconscious.

Some lowbrow writers go out of their way to create rigidly even speech.[10] They avoid common contractions, for example, and other speech mannerisms which middlebrow and highbrow writers use to distinguish among speakers.[11] Uniform speech patterns of social equals mark a sameness among lowbrow characters. Bakhtin explains that highbrow novels do the opposite: they use highly marked distinctions to identify individual speakers and to display how others relate as "other."[12]

Lowbrow novels typically begin with an episode from which the main character is absent or involved with someone who becomes relatively unimportant to the plot (consider Scarlett O'Hara and the Tarleton twins). This scene enables readers to see the parameters of the world the character must perform in: we learn mores, precepts, potential enemies and allies, and social peculiarities, all of which encourage us to play the role of judge in deciding whether the character is making good choices in a given set of circumstances. Robert L. Root says that, since genre fiction must "adhere to conventions or deflate readers' expectations," they "declare their ethos on the first page."[13]

In Frank Slaughter's *The Healer* the first pages focus on registered nurse Trudy Foster opening up Dr. Donald Carter's office for the day and reflecting on the good life she has spent serving the doctor and his predecessor, mentor, benefactor, and surrogate father (Carter is an orphan), Dr. Henry Bolton. Trudy is the moral yardstick of the novel: Carter had better carry on the practices that have heretofore made life satisfying for this selfless unmarried woman.

Metalious's *Peyton Place* opens onto the town's pundits bringing the week to a close: Doc Swain and newspaper publisher Seth Buswell exchange quips about the terrors of organized religion; assorted men watching the town drunk meander home allow that "There ain't much a feller can do when he's married to a born whore."[14]

Schoolteacher Miss Elsie Thornton dismisses her pupils and momentarily despairs that "she has fought a losing battle with ignorance," but remembers her commitment that "If I can . . . awaken in only one child a sense of beauty . . . an admission of ignorance and a thirst for knowledge, then I am fulfilled." Allison Mackenzie is her designated protegé, the child who must rise above the limitations of this environment—through education rather than religion—to keep the likes of Elsie Thornton from despairing.

Lowbrow protagonists enter the limelight to wage battles they are ill-equipped to win, which often threaten their identity or jeopardize their social position. Typically, they are made to leave home, deprived of parental guidance, faced with visceral temptation, and/or unprovokedly put upon by the forces of evil, sometimes in the form of rivals and enemies who try to snare them into immoral, rash, and ruinous behavior.

This plot, very much like the fairy tale plot outlined by Bettelheim, contains five requirements: the protagonist must 1. leave home; 2. forego immediate gratification; 3. take risks; 4. submit to trials and accept aid; 5. meet the demands of an assistant (133). Radway's account (134) and Cawelti's (39-40) contain similar features.[15] Cawelti's also contains a theme from Northrop Frye's romance structure—that the hero must ascend after a descent into the realm of death or chaos.

In Slaughter's novel Dr. Carter's situation is typically full of rivals, enemies, and temptations. Since Bolton's death Carter (rather than Bolton's son, also a physician but an unskilled and unscrupulous one) has become the "old man" of Bolton Clinic, responsible for maintaining its humanitarian practices. The disinherited son aims to ruin Carter by providing legal services for a family that wants to sue him for malpractice. While trying to obtain a divorce from Bolton's daughter (a spendthrift and a drunk), Carter falls in love with his new young, affianced surgical assistant, Laura Jordan.

When an unlikely-to-succeed emergency brain tumor operation results in the patient's death, Carter fears that his infatuation with Laura caused him to err in surgery. But before he can disconfirm this possibility, Laura (the only person who could have witnessed the error if he had made it), is knocked down by a wayward truck and left amnesiac. This is Carter's risk: he is the only surgeon who might cure her, but he knows that to do so might restore her memory of a surgical mistake that would end his career. As the book cover asks: "Should he save the life of a woman who might ruin him?"[16]

To overcome antagonistic forces, lowbrow protagonists must learn to take risks which usually require sacrificing the *self* to another person or for a worthier cause. In male novels these sacrifices translate into risking one's life. For example, the soldier bravely faces enemy fire to contribute to a meaningful war effort, or the detective risks the snares of devious criminals in order to control crime, or Dr. Carter risks the career that is his life. (I'm using the terms "male novels" and "female novels" in discussing lowbrow fiction because, as I said in chapter one, lowbrow novels often segregate their readerships by gender.[17])

In female novels, the ubiquitous equivalent is yielding up one's virginity or "virtue" to a male who appears to be worthy of that prize—in other words, entering holy matrimony. Because yielding to men is the plot device that attracts so much criticism to women's fiction, I think we need to regard it as a symbolic counterpart to male heroism and an example of self-sacrifice.[18] Tania Modleski sees the marriage that ends the typical romance as part of Frye's "descent" motif, but suggests that to readers the ceremony marks the promise of ascent: "I'll die, but I'll be back!"[19]

Our culture doesn't have an adequate alternative symbol for female selflessness. The examples that come to mind—the spinster teacher who devotes her life to her pupils (William Gibson's *The Miracle Worker*); the mother who gives up sleep, food, and all material assets for her children (Fanny Hurst's *Imitation of Life*)—do make up powerful and popular literature. But they tend toward hagiography: they require saintly personalities or special gifts and consequently fall outside essential bounds of lowbrow fiction. Any male has a life to give up and any female her virtue; therefore, these are acts available to any reader, who may very well intuit that risking personal safety for someone else's sake is what these novels are about rather than explicit acts of bravery or sexual submission. Maybe the pattern of reward for self-sacrifice explains why women of all ages and phases of personal sexual relationships read women's romances and male novels of any description.

Taking risks, learning to discern who is trustworthy, accepting assistance, being resourceful, industrious, and patient, and welcoming licit relations with an appropriate member of the opposite sex comprise a kind of charter or code of law by which lowbrow protagonists must abide if they are to overcome obstacles and lead happy lives.[20] While the basic charter remains consistent, its particular stipulations alter to suit changing social conditions.

The serialized romance *Lonesome Road*[21] shows how lowbrow novels reflect changes in social code, for, in a very fifties scheme, risking premarital sex becomes the *moral* option when it is motivated by "true love." The heroine has to give up high school and a lead in the class play and endure a pregnancy while her lover is called off to war. But these sacrifices are trivial in contrast to the unhappy marriage her sister suffers because she rejected her true love when he insisted that they have sex before marriage. Though *Lonesome Road* is a cartoon strip compared to Richardson's *Pamela*, both these novels resemble moral fables that display culturally constructed sexual mores.

In *Lonesome Road*, as in *Peyton Place*, the woman who "teaches us what not to be" is a secondary character. In a more realistic lowbrow novel of the fifties, the heroine of *Home Before Dark*,[22] is made to suffer a mental collapse and the dissolution of her marriage to show what happens to protagonists who don't hold out against temptation or who willfully break codes. Charlotte Bronn's jealousy of a rival woman led her to "trap" her husband rather than let "nature take its course." She wins marriage, but must give up her musical goals and talents to try to be the kind of wife her husband wants. Inevitably, she loses the struggle anyway. The novel implies that a marriage contrived and not made in heaven is destined to bring misery and loneliness rather than love and self-fulfillment.

Jim Bledsoe, protagonist of *Run Silent, Run Deep*,[23] fails his first trial run as commander of a submarine when he puts desire for glory and power above his responsibility as attentive and faithful husband. He learns restraint and becomes a decorated commander and a proper husband, but the two transgressions are enough to cause him to end up "deep-sixed." He's redeemed himself for the next life, perhaps, but not this one. At novel's end it appears that his long-suffering and beautiful widow will be courted by the more mature narrator, Sgt. Richardson.

Middlebrow novels have less predictable plot turns and more cleverly camouflaged functional characters. They are most recognizable by precision and a plethora of mimetic detail. Terry Lovell says that authenticity of realism requires lengthy description which fantasy does not.[24] Middlebrow novels tend to be longer on the average, with more characters and more biographical description of even minor characters.

Language is more artful, figurative and elaborate than in lowbrow novels, but less subtle and more self-conscious than in highbrow. Figures of speech, symbols, and details draw attention to themselves. For example, in *From Here to Eternity*, Warden, who is neither bookish nor religious, says to Prewitt, "I'm only the instrument of a laughing Providence."[25] Prewitt's name, Robert E. Lee Prewitt, ponderously symbolizes a doomed crusader. When highbrow writers use tipnames, they make fun of themselves in the process. In Ralph Ellison's *Invisible Man*, the false-hearted black college president, Bledsoe, preaches on Julius Caesar; a traitorous official in the Brotherhood is named Wrestrum. Why the difference? Perhaps because, in spite of the necessity for realism, middlebrow novelists have to identify their medium as a ritual in service of a public good, a language construct that should not be taken as ordinary speech.

Since a main function of the middlebrow novel is to convince its readers that oppressive social strictures are manageable (in the same manner that myths do according to Lévi-Strauss's concept of myth-work[26]), readers must be assured that the circumstances characters deal with accurately mimic the real world. These novels must also show that idiosyncrasies of character rather than the vagaries of the external world are what give the middlebrow protagonist trouble and effect hopes for success.

The typical middlebrow opening features an aspect of the protagonist's background or personality with inherent potential for conflict with a social system. Kay's anxious ambition comes through in the opening of Mary McCarthy's *The Group*:

> It was June, 1933, one week after Commencement, when Kay Leiland Strong, Vassar '33, the first of her class to run around the table at the Class Day dinner, was married to Harald Petersen, Reed, '27, in the chapel of St. George's Church, P.E., Karl F. Reiland, Rector.[27]

Prewitt's rigidity shows in the opening of *From Here to Eternity*:

> When he finished packing, he walked out on to the third-floor porch of the barracks brushing the dust from his hands, a very neat and deceptively slim young man in the summer khakis that were still early morning fresh. (9)

Sloan Wilson's *Man in the Gray Flannel Suit* begins:

> By the time they had lived seven years in the little house on
> Greentree Avenue in Westport, Connecticut, they both detested
> it. . . . For one thing, the house had a kind of evil genius for dis-
> playing proof of their weaknesses and wiping out all traces of
> their strengths. The ragged lawn and weed-filled garden pro-
> claimed to passers-by and neighbors that Thomas R. Rath and his
> family disliked "working around the place" and couldn't afford
> to pay someone else to do it. (1)

A clash with institutions is suggested in each of these openings:
Kay expects marriage to be as fine and flashy as the credentials in that
opening sentence; Prewitt's sense of personal integrity (signaled by his
obsessive neatness) and his repressed hostility (the "deceptive slimness"
that hides the boxer's taut body) suggest his inability to adapt himself to
the less-than-honorable army he has enlisted in; everything about the
opening of Wilson's book, including Tom Rath's name, suggests inadequate enterprise and latent hostility against a system that does not automatically fulfill desires.

As in Thomas Hardy's, "The Convergence of the Twain,"[28] and
great myths such as *Oedipus Rex*,[29] one force that is beyond human control and one whose control is threatened by human vanity embark on a
collision course. Unlike the contests of lowbrow fiction to see if the
"good self" can overcome the "bad self," middlebrow plots pit the
hero's private wishes to enhance or maintain status against public strictures (in mythic terms, embedded social structure such as the power of
the Delphic Oracle; in modern terms, "the system") which will not be
modified by the hero's desires. The protagonist is required to rework
priorities, thereby making the most common question of a middlebrow
novel some version of "What price glory?"[30]

In an early forerunner of the middlebrow novel, Robinson
Crusoe[31] desires to take advantage of new opportunities for adventure
and the amassing of personal fortune by signing on as a merchant sea-
man. His defiance of the private order—Christian obedience to his
father's request that he remain at home—obstructs his freedom to do
what pleases him.

The breach of the private ethic is followed by Crusoe's being
stranded on an uninhabited island, the sole survivor of a shipwreck. To cut
his losses Crusoe must adapt himself to the ethic he has transgressed,
which he accomplishes by becoming skilled at field and animal hus-
bandry, patience and piety—values threatened by changes in eighteenth-

century civil order. This exchange illustrates the middlebrow ethic that one can salvage some contentment in a changing order by assiduously cultivating those features which seem most endangered.[32]

In 1719, the early edge of the modern era (when moral systems have become recognizable as social constructs rather than natural laws), it would make sense that the private system should be the one that constrains rather than supports as it does in the 1950s. By mid-twentieth century, the apprehension is that social institutions overrule private morality. Tom Rath also desires to capitalize on opportunities for personal advancement, but unlike Crusoe, the Raths would like to live by their private ethic and are forced by the social ethic to betray it. Dickstein's unwillingness to declare *Robinson Crusoe* a novel may stem from the contrast that Tom can learn to compromise in order to cut his losses, whereas Crusoe's losses are inflicted upon him before he has a chance to compromise.[33]

Perhaps because of the need to illustrate opportunities and options for compromise, middlebrow plot structures are more varied than lowbrow (one is also tempted to say more strung out, since they lack the efficient dynamism of a denouement determined by a specific test). Some develop two or more stories simultaneously, so that readers see various sets of characters operating in the same social milieu and get a bird's eye view of the momentum of various forces. *The Group*, for example, examines various ways of dealing with one institution by focusing on the romantic lives of several Vassar girls. Marriage, rather than being a comfortable compromise, is always a source of discomfort.

Kay Strong Petersen labors to make an unlikely marriage ideal: she spends the money she thinks she and Harald ought to have, pushes him to accomplish more than he's inclined to, holds him up to other's standards of how often they should have sex and what kind of parties and furnishings they should have, and ends up with a nervous breakdown and a divorce. Another McCarthy character who tries to live by the book is Priss Hartshorn Crockett. Though Priss has almost no milk, her physician-husband insists she breast-feed their son Stephen on an absolutely regular schedule. This regimen results in a neurotic mother and a neurotic child.

The least-troubled characters are those who never marry, though both pay a price for this, Polly by losing her compatible and satisfying lover Gus when he decides to return to his wife, and Lakey by having to become something of an exile in Europe, where her lesbianism is more accepted. In effect, the book is a catalog of life-style options complete with warning labels about the concomitant hazards of each: *caveat emptor.*

Middlebrow novels like Helen Howe's *Circle of the Day* engage protagonist Faith Millett in a wide variety of experiences which enable her to size up her situation. A phone call from a catty friend early in the morning of her tenth wedding anniversary informs Millett that the life she thought perfect is smirched: her husband has fathered a child by another woman during the war. Her decision to begin divorce proceedings is heartily commended by a cynical dowager she meets at her hairdresser's. But a variety of ensuing encounters give her a more seasoned perspective.

These include contrast (a friend who's contemplating divorce), options (an old flame who remains an irresponsible hedonist), a "mirror" (a warning from her daughter's gym teacher that Faith is over-protective), and biography (her dying mother-in-law's confession that Eric spent an unhappy boyhood because she could not bring herself to show him affection after his father died). Toward evening, she walks by Gramercy Park to get a glimpse of Eric's boy—a "beautiful child." And, as if all this isn't enough, she witnesses a fatal auto accident. Together these experiences move Faith not to jeopardize the happiness of others to achieve her own brand of contentment.

Whether it presents multiple viewpoints or multifarious circumstances, the middlebrow novel preaches that the conditions of the world require compromise: happiness is never absolute, and, if you can't accept that, there are worse consequences to suffer. To convince readers that they are getting a dependable instance of life—to allow them to use their novel-reading as survival training, mimetic naturalism is a stock feature of middlebrow novels.

Highbrow novels reject the principle that right courses of action are knowable; therefore, highbrow fiction works hard to undermine mimetic naturalism. Language, plotting, and characterization serve to defamiliarize the highbrow world. Linguistic play is in some sense its very essence, for by using language that demands attention to the process of decoding, highbrow writers signal that whatever appears on the page is a mere construct of language, not a means to an end but an end in itself. Humbert's monologue at the opening of Lolita foregrounds this strategy:

> Lolita, light of my life, fire of my loins. My sin, my soul. Lo-lee-ta: the tip of the tongue taking a trip of three steps down the palate to tap, at three, on the teeth. Lo. Lee. Ta. . . .
> Did she have a precursor? Indeed she did. In point of fact, there might have been no Lolita at all had I not loved, one summer, a certain initial girl-child. In a princedom by the sea. Oh

when? About as many years before Lolita was born as my age
was that summer. You can always count on a murderer for a
fancy prose style.
   Ladies and gentlemen of the jury, exhibit number one is
what the seraphs, the misinformed, simple, noble-winged seraphs, envied. Look at this tangle of thorns. (11)

Nabokov's soliloquizing, alliteration, and allusion to Poe are
both obvious and fanciful. The passage is one of many that warn the
reader that this is not realism.
   Though less manic, the opening monologue in Bellow's
Henderson the Rain King, still signals (through the juxtaposition of
banality and poetry—"my teeth" and "all is grief") that this rush of anxiety is fictionalized:

When I think of my condition at the age of fifty-five when I
bought the ticket, all is grief. . . . A disorderly rush begins—my
parents, my wives, my girls, my children, my farm, my animals,
my habits, my money, my music lessons, my drunkenness, my
prejudices, my brutality, my teeth, my face, my soul![34]

Highbrow novels also quickly apprise readers that the characters
they're dealing with are not to be taken as real people. In Wallace
Martin's words, highbrow novelists "defamiliarize through 'unusual
eyes.'"[35] Purdy's *Malcolm* opens with the startling detail that fifteen-
year-old Malcolm has been sitting all day long for days on a "golden
parkbench" awaiting his father's return; Malamud's *The Assistant* hints
at peculiarity in Bober's obsessive attention to transactions that would
be inconsequential to an ordinary grocer—delaying important chores in
order to ring up a three-cent sale, fretting over the absence of a customer
who usually spent thirty cents, changing a credit slip from $2.03 to
$1.61 so that his wife wouldn't get angry about the credit.[36]
   The highbrow novel protagonist has neither to learn how to actu-
alize the "good self" nor how to adapt to the demands of an unaccom-
modating world, but to figure out what the world *is* in order to find a
place in it. Again, this generalization is truer of fifties highbrow than
that of previous or succeeding generations.
   Two broad strains of highbrow novels exist in America: those in
the Hawthorne/Melville tradition of the search for the true nature of the
human being and those in the Twain/James tradition of the search for the
true nature of our social selves. The former exploit the folklore tradition

and deconstruct it to reveal that the holy grail is a leaky bucket. The latter exploit novel conventions themselves (like Lawrence Sterne's *Tristram Shandy*) by discrediting their truth-telling ability and continually pointing out the generation of text and creation of story. What these strains share with fifties highbrow novels is the premise that without novels such as these we see only "through a glass darkly"—misidentify our own and others' motivations.

The eponymous hero of *Tristram Shandy* is one of the world's earliest examples of a hero on a quest to fathom the nature of the world. Having deduced that he himself is the product of some sort of clockwork machination wrought by his punctilious father and that all humans are somehow caught up in private "hobby-horses," as is his Uncle Toby, Tristram determines not to take himself too seriously.

Fifties highbrow protagonists have less organized lives from which to learn appropriate attitudes and roles. Malcolm spends his days sitting on the parkbench outside the hotel where he and his father had been staying because he has no idea of what else to do—no instructions, no guardians, no home or family to return to. A self-appointed mentor and the variety of individuals he introduces Malcolm to, who wish to adopt him, train him, or otherwise provide for him, are less than helpful: they give ambiguous, disconcerting, and self-serving assistance. The world Malcolm discovers is a world without a father and without traditional authority, charter, or pervasive ethic to prescribe effective behavior. It is the inverse of the world of lowbrow fiction.

In Nabokov's novel, Lolita learns that the father who replaces the one she's lost is no father, just as Humbert Humbert learns how easy it is to distance himself from the responsibility of fatherhood. Their cross-country odyssey is a journey to look upon that which is not: there are no walls to scale, no enemy to conquer, no Penelope weaving at home, no Telemachus waiting in the wings. The look into that "wasteland" makes comprehensible Lolita's option to tie herself into a version of stability by marrying a local boy, having a baby, and settling into a clapboard house in a tacky suburb—like so many of her real-life fifties counterparts—and yet also renders that solution a figment of Humbert's imagining.

Once the familiar has been made strange, the highbrow novel requires the protagonist and/or reader to invent a new charter and/or discredit an old one in order to endure or thrive in this new world. *Tristram Shandy* gives this job to the reader by marking the character's naiveté and his worldly conditions as authorial contrivance, by making a careful organization look like confusion, and by speaking through an "intruding narrator"[37] who gives "equivocal testimony."[38] In *On the Road*, Kerouac gives the job to Sal Paradise. Sal is set up as kind of an inexperienced "mama's boy" incapable of seeing how self-serving the "heroic" Dean Moriarty is until he leaves Sal virtually dying of dysentery on a Mexican desert.

Since nothing is what it seems to be, the lesson of the highbrow novel is perception: highbrow novels demonstrate *how* to look at the world rather than what there is to see. Reading *Tristram Shandy* does not leave a reader with a sense of having observed an individual life, as, say, *From Here to Eternity* might, but of having observed how an individual might perceive life. It is not an individual's circumstances that inform the reader but the consciousness that registers those circumstances.

And that consciousness is foregrounded by means of putting the "real world" out of focus. Sterne uses incongruous humor to distort the real world focus; Nabokov uses a "perverted" narrator; Bellow uses a fantastical setting and a larger than life character. In contrast to the "average" protagonists of lowbrow fiction, characters of unusual dimension or accomplishment typically populate highbrow fiction (think of Rabbit, who is always mindful of his glory days as a basketball star, of his height and his girth, of Captain Ahab, of Raskolnikov).

The double vision of both Jewish grocer Morris Bober and Italian ex-con Frank Alpine obscures the focus of *The Assistant*. Readers are made to ask: For what reasons does Bober harbor a criminal in his basement? Does he seek his own punishment for an ill-spent life? Does he sacrifice himself for Frank's redemption? Is he making a pact with the devil to repay a nagging wife? Is Frank a devil? Is any of his reclamative behavior—working endless hours for virtually no wages, creating new and successful business schemes, working an extra job to help finance Helen's education, getting circumcised and becoming a Jew—anything but manipulative and self-serving? Can Frank love the same girl that he rapes? Can he honor the same man that he cudgels?

Rather than answer these questions, *The Assistant* thrusts them at the reader, so that all personal, communal, and stereotypical notions of maturity, honor, and altruism are jeopardized. The charter which describes correct and incorrect behavior is neither discovered (lowbrow) nor revised (middlebrow). Rather, the possibility of such a charter is essentially denied—a contrast which aligns the highbrow novel more with the lowbrow than the middlebrow novel.

Both highbrow and lowbrow protagonists begin life in search of charters (often in the form of "fathers," as in the cases of Allison

MacKenzie and Frank Alpine) or in the grasp of false charters (Constance and Humbert Humbert). In lowbrow novels the charter works because humans and human institutions work according to a consistent description. Highbrow novels deconstruct these descriptions, showing them to be contradictory or fallacious because they cannot be applied even-handedly to myriad and unstable situations and because the characters themselves are conflicted.

In middlebrow novels the charter can work because of the expectation that imperfect human beings can adapt themselves to imperfect social institutions. Order is first denied in the middlebrow novel by the failure of institutions to keep up their end of the bargain, but the novel proceeds to demonstrate that institutions are not obliged to; in a Darwinian (and mythical) sense, systems are looked at as naturally evolved by the necessities of survival. Therefore, it behooves the middlebrow protagonist to adapt himself to a world with new rules.

But this "domination-affirming" feature of middlebrow novels is not necessarily debilitating to novel readers. There is something life-affirming about these novels—if we acknowledge that we read novels to find out about the strength of human beings, not the strength of institutions (knowledge that we're probably already well sated with via other media anyway).

It seems likely that in our reading we are looking for some affirmation that we're capable of defending ourselves against an imperfect order or at least surviving within it. Where lowbrow novels assert the human capacity to be selfless, middlebrow novels assert our capacity for self-preservation. Highbrow novels assert our capacity to be canny, unique, and self-sufficient.

What these differences spell out are clearly distinct world views in lowbrow, middlebrow and highbrow novels. The fictional world that lowbrow readers envision is consistent, knowable, familiar, and equitable. It is populated by characters who resemble their readers in basic creeds and wishes. It rewards the "good" and punishes the "bad." Highbrow readers move into a world that is inconsistent, unfamiliar and at best impartial, populated by characters who are separated from their readers by unique creeds and wishes. "Good" and "bad" are unknowable factors in this world, but their elusiveness is a constant stimulus. Middlebrow readers find a world that is familiar but inconsistent, knowable but immoral. Its characters are fallible human beings who will survive or succumb depending on their capacity to redefine "the good life" and to adapt their creeds and wishes to new circumstances.

Lowbrow, middlebrow, and highbrow novels are componentially distinct, rather than items on a continuum. Each provides different kinds of pleasures and challenges to their readers. Each affirms characteristics about the world that need affirming for these readers. My insistence on this separateness is not meant to indicate that these levels form a scale of quality or value, anymore than dogs, cats, and canaries form a scale of quality pets.

I do see all subgenres of the novel serving the same general functions for readers: providing sources of peace and contentment, adventure, vicarious sexual pleasure, ego gratification, imaginary means for defeating "the forces of evil," and perhaps others.

I think the various levels challenge concepts of self and social relationships in ways that readers who select them are willing to have such concepts challenged. Part of our reading pleasure involves putting ourselves (our sense of self-worth, our value systems, our creeds) at risk—much as we do when we shove off down a ski slope or step behind the lectern in a classroom. But we only take that risk when we have some assurance that a good deal of what we risk will be returned to us intact—just as we don't ski unless we believe that we can handle the slopes, nor teach unless we think we'll be able to field the questions students ask.

It seems clear that when readers reject highbrow novels they are declining to have some things jeopardized—their confidence in an orderly universe or the innate goodness of human beings, or their ability to read. But readers who reject lowbrow novels are declining risks also—of getting "lost" in a book or of embracing communal ethics.

NOTES

1. See Janice Radway, *Reading the Romance* (Chapel Hill: U of North Carolina P, 1984), 5-6, and John G. Cawelti, *Adventure, Mystery, and Romance: Formula Stories as Art and Popular Culture* (Chicago: U of Chicago P, 1976), 5-80.

2. Vladimir Propp says of folktale structure that nothing is out of sequence, setting is always where the hero acts, and nothing is told from an alternate point of view. *Morphology of a Folktale*, trans. Laurence Scott (Austin: U of Texas P, 1968), 22-23.

3. Kathleen Winsor (New York: Macmillan, 1944).

4. *Love's $weet Return: The Harlequin Story* (Toronto: Women's, 1984), 93.

5. Nicholas Parsons, *The Book of Literary Lists* (New York and Oxford: Facts on File, 1987), 90.

6. (New York: Pantheon, 1960), 336.

7. Barbara Hinckley and Karen Hinckley, *American Best Sellers* (Bloomington: Indiana UP, 1989), 145.

8. Review of Colleen McCullough's, *The First Man in Rome*, *Minneapolis Star Tribune* 7 Oct. 1990: f11.

9. Hinckley, 4.

10. See examples and discussion of James Jones's dialogue in chapter five and Mickey Spillane's in chapter eight.

11. Hans Robert Jauss suggests in his discussion of medieval romances that a "middle style" affected by courtly speech suggested its function of mediating between the boundaries of "other world" fiction and an ordered social life. *Toward an Aesthetic of Reception*, trans. Timothy Bahti; *Theory and History of Literature*, 2 (Minneapolis, U of Minnesota P, 1982), 83-87.

12. Mikhail Bakhtin, *Rabelais and his World*, trans. Helene Iswolsky (Cambridge, MA: MIT P. 1968), 361.

13. *The Rhetorics of Popular Culture: Advertising, Advocacy, and Entertainment* (New York: Greenwood, 1987), 138.

14. Grace Metalious, *Peyton Place* (New York: Pocket Books, 1956), 6. Further quotations will be cited from this edition.

15. Radway's is more detailed as is Propp's: Radway's has 13 steps; Propp's, 30.

16. Frank G. Slaughter, *The Healer* (1955; New York: Pocket, 1967), front cover.

17. Flynn and Schweickart point out that reading "as a male" implies "maintaining ego and text boundaries," whereas reading "as a female" implies "experiencing a world that seems unnarrated" (xxiv-xxv). Though Flynn and Schweickart don't draw this conclusion, other reading studies suggest that women learn to read "like men" when they deal with "non-female" texts. The contrast also suggests a reason why women's popular fiction is more widely feared than men's—because women seem to "disappear" into the texts as they read. See Tania Modleski, "The Disappearing Act," *Signs: Journal of Women in Culture and Society* 5 (1980), 435-48.

18. Cawelti supports this in suggesting that the romance is the female equivalent of the adventure story (41).

19. *Loving with a Vengeance: Mass-Produced Fantasies for Women* (Hamden, CT: Archon, 1982), 48.

20. Bettelheim, 35.

21. Anne Wormer, in *Redbook* (Nov. 1953), 121-52.

22. Eileen Bassing (New York: Random, 1957).

23. Edward L. Beach (New York: Pocket Books, 1955).

24. *Consuming Fictions* (London: Verso, 1987), 8.

25. James Jones, *From Here to Eternity* (New York: New American Library, 1951), 52. All further quotations will be cited from this edition.

26. See chapters three and six.

27. (1954; New York: Signet), 1963, 7. Notice that McCarthy's readers are expected to know the significance of "run around the table."

28. In this poem (1913), Hardy narrates the progress of two "construction jobs": God's building of an iceburg in the depths of the north Atlantic and the Star Company's building of an "unsinkable" ship and the eventual "convergence of the twain" in which one must succumb to the strength of the other.

29. I am grateful to Michael Hancher for pointing out this comparison.

30. Bettelheim explains that in mythical stories the hero aspires to victory over others, in fairy tales to victory over the self (199).

31. Dickstein argues that Crusoe is too laconic and unemotional to be a novel's hero (48), but I use the book because its capitalistic underpinnings make it more than an adventure yarn or survival manual. Crusoe's struggle with economic rather than social success makes it a middlebrow novel.

32. Ian Watt, *The Rise of the Novel* (Berkeley: U of California P, 1964). This fact may also explain why the nuclear family is so hallowed by fifties popular culture; as we can see from a nineties perspective, its sanctity was doomed.

33. The "cut your losses" theme is particularly fifties, for this is an era of losses (of roots, values, family, insularity). "Survival through solidarity" might better describe the theme of thirties' middlebrow novels like Steinbeck's *Grapes of Wrath* and *In Dubious Battle*, wherein cutting one's losses involved finding support and compassion from others similarly abused by the system. *An American Tragedy, Babbitt, Main Street* of the twenties show the era's preoccupation with molding ourselves into socially constructed images, and cutting losses required deconstructing those images. Classic middlebrows of the forties, on the other hand, suggest a retreat to conventionality as the means to cut the losses inflicted by war and depression (easier to see in the decade's films, in which many critics have noted the retreat to conventional sex-role notions and show liberated women full of fear about not being able to take care of themselves.

34. Saul Bellow (New York: Avon, 1958), 7.

35. "*Recent Theories of Narrative* (Ithaca: Cornell UP, 1986), 49.

36. Bernard Malamud, *The Assistant* (New York: Avon, 1957), 1-2.

37. Wayne C. Booth, "The Self-Conscious Narrator in Prose Fiction," *PMLA* 67 (1952), 163-64.

38. William Bowman Piper, "Tristram Shandy's Tragicomical Testimony," *Criticism* 3.3 (1961): 171.

V

FACING WAR IN FIFTIES FICTION

The subjects of war and the military reveal how the subgenres differ in their treatment of contemporary circumstances. Lowbrow, middlebrow, and highbrow writers employ differing mechanisms for coping with similar external conditions. Lowbrow shows a capacity for recycling standard themes through whatever materials are at hand;[1] middlebrow, for making adaptation the responsibility of the individual; and highbrow, for making history another factor in the individual's fight against depersonalization.

And each responds to historical conditions in a way modified by the ethos of the American fifties. One should expect that middlebrow novels will reveal the most about their connection to the fifties, since middlebrow novels particularly mimic conditions of the time of the writing. They attend to problematic conditions and question societal norms.

The lowbrow novel treats societal norms like the Ten Commandments: Characters may be judged wrong or bad for going against them, but the norms themselves are never questioned. The highbrow novel may confront societal norms, but generally only those that impinge upon self-awareness or individual identity. Though the highbrow novel aims to strip the reader of illusions, authors generally focus on illusions characters have about themselves rather than illusions about the nature of our institutions, in order not to distract from the highbrow struggle toward self-actualization.

Because war entangles the superego of civilization with the id of self-preservation, war novels show rather graphically the "middling" function of middlebrow novels. The lowbrow novel hypervaluates the superego of civilization; highbrow hypervaluates self-preservation; middlebrow aims to strike the happy medium. Middlebrow protagonists, as the following discussion will show, attempt to attain stature, success, and dignity in the military without obliterating their own egos.

In any generation, the egos of men at war are threatened by death, deprivation, the absolute authority of commanding officers, and a need to justify destructive acts. The fifties stamped these issues with a challenged patriotism, a skeptical attitude toward authority, and increasing secularization. Take away the notions that dying in battle will guarantee a higher berth in the afterlife or that he should be happy to escape this "veil of tears," and a soldier may wonder what he's missing out on while he's taking orders from someone dumber than he who's eating better rations. Perhaps these changes occurred because media displayed warfare's savagery, because we knew we couldn't "make the world safe for democracy," or because the chance to live a good life seemed so much more likely after the Depression.[2]

The power of officers became a particular problem in the postwar era and its fiction. Universal education, perhaps, or the mass media had informed us that within the military establishment, as in business and industry, the privileged, the aggressive, and the opportunistic got ahead. Middlebrow war novels confront these misgivings with "brutally honest" depictions of the historical or institutional conditions. The impact is nonetheless minimized by focusing attention on characters' need to adapt to a unique moment in history. The facts of war and the military are made the background against which the character must check excesses and develop expediencies of behavior in order not to be done in. In the world of the middlebrow novel history elapses; institutions evolve; people adapt. Situations are negotiable; proper behavior is pragmatic.

The character of Hearn in Mailer's powerfully written *The Naked and the Dead* shows how institutional corruption becomes a tertiary issue. Hearn is the intellectual and moral superior of Cummings and Croft, officers who outrank him. He loses to them not because they're buttressed by a corrupt power structure, but because he refuses to play their games: he deliberately leaves a cigarette butt on his office floor to antagonize Cummings, and, though he knows that Croft will do anything to maintain control over his platoon, Hearn fails to provide himself a cover as he walks into the trap Croft has set for him.

Mailer's novel is middlebrow because Mailer creates a less-than-indifferent battlefield in *The Naked and the Dead*, by undoing the corrupt intentions of Croft and Cummings with "poetically just" fortuities. Cummings's plot to impress his superiors by taking Anapopei is satirically undone when he absents himself for a day to deliberate with superiors.

His subordinate, who knows nothing of Cummings's strategies (let alone strategizing of any kind), is forced to direct an unexpected battle and "masterminds" the *coup de guerre* by sheer chance. Croft's foolhardy self-promotion fails when his reconnaissance troops stumble into a hornet's nest that catapults the entire company down the mountainside.

Bo, the hero of John Hersey's *The War Lover*, sees the need to readjust his expectations rather than count on the army to control the increasing insanity of the "war lover" who pilots Bo's bomber crew. To shake off his despair and make his participation in war bearable, Bo must establish new priorities. In this case that means hoping that dumb luck will offset the threatening heroics of a brilliant but power-mad pilot.

In the middlebrow novel there is always some way out for the character that doesn't involve a restructuring of the institution, but more likely of the characters' principles. James Jones's *From Here to Eternity* offers this kind of options. Jones exposes the corruptions of the modern army, its wastefulness, capriciousness, and sloth; yet he makes the protagonist not so much victim of these problems as his own worst enemy.

Robert E. Lee Prewitt is given a slate of characteristics guaranteed to clash endlessly with the weaknesses of the modern army. These include pride, "bolshevism," ignorance, backwoods upbringing, perfectionism, and enough brains and skill to recognize and resent authority figures with much less. He's a minor-league Hercules without the gods on his side. He becomes the army's sparring partner, and, deprived of its measure of clout, he needs to muster all his wits in order to survive each round. But Prewitt relies on outmoded ethics rather than brains.

Like Mailer, Jones sees the military hierarchy as corrupted by power. Jones's Brigadier General Sam Slater shows what Prewitt is up against when he complains that " 'Honor, Patriotism, and Service,' " no longer exist in the army and "the fear of authority which was once only a side issue . . . is the main issue. . . [T]he lot of modern man has become . . . 'perpetual apprehension.' "[3]

The worst abuse of power happens within the stockade run by Major Thompson, who believes that "the quickest, efficientest, least expensive way to educate a man is to make it painful for him when he is wrong, the same as with any other animal" (510). His aide-de-camp, S/Sgt. "Fatso" Judson, supports his philosophy by inflicting bone-breaking punishment for infractions as minor as a poorly arranged shelf.

Jones's army is as corrupt as Mailer's, but his characters continue to believe that they can somehow thrive within its structure. Prewitt and Warden have both dedicated their lives to the army—which Jones often reminds us they have great reverence for—and conscientiously try to maintain a self-defined measure of integrity without getting shut down by the system.[4] Both Warden and Prewitt know that some features of the army are immutable.

Warden, for example, resists applying for a commission because he believes that "Being an officer would make a son of a bitch out of Christ himself"(51). Buddies who caution Prewitt against his urge to kill S/Sgt. Judson argue that he is "a part of the army you love" and "they'll get somebody just like him to replace him"(630). Warden's character shows what degree of satisfaction a man might attain by playing along with the system wherever it is necessary; Prewitt demonstrates what degree of self-determination is self-destructive.

Through the course of the novel Prewitt makes a series of choices which underscore his unwillingness to adjust his personal requirements when the system does not suit him. These lead inevitably to his being shot as a fleeing deserter. As the book opens Prewitt has applied for a transfer, in order to express his anger at his company commander for assigning someone else to be head bugler (perhaps because the officer has homosexual interests in the less talented bugler).[5] The move entails being busted to private, docked in pay, and required to perform routine army chores. Accepting a spot in Holmes's "jockstrap" division compounds his jeopardy, for Prewitt knows that Holmes will be especially anxious for him, a former welterweight champion, to box on the company team. Prewitt also knows that he won't box. He quit fighting when he blinded a sparring partner and then renewed a death-bed oath to his mother to never hurt anyone unnecessarily.[6]

His resolve to tough it out collapses when the obsequious immigrant Sgt. Ike Galovitch upbraids him in front of Capt. Holmes for not working hard enough at fatigue clean up. To Galovitch's remonstrance (" 'You, Prewitt, lets looking a life. Dis a fatigue, not vacation for a seminary of lady' "), Prewitt retorts: " 'What the hell do you want, me to grow a couple more arms for Chrissake?' " (273).

What saves him from the stockade this time is Warden's reminder to Holmes that Prewitt's sentence would correspond with boxing season. But Prewitt is not so lucky a month later when Ike attacks him with a knife. The knife plunges into a crack in a concrete slab as Ike falls into a drunken stupor (484-5).

His attorney assures him that he'll get a light sentence if he pleads guilty, but Prewitt perversely refuses: "I aint guilty. And I aint going to plead guilty. Not even if it would mean a full acquittal." His lawyer explodes: "What has that got to do with it? Nobody gives a damn whether you're guilty or not. The court doesn't care" (493-4).

First-hand experience of the stockade and Judson's sadistic tactics cement Prewitt's intent to kill him—a decision that confirms Jones's image of Prewitt as self-destructive. He does show some will to survive in planning the murder: He buys a standard issue switchblade, waits an intentionally indifferent nine days after his release from the stockade, and attacks Judson after dark in the alley behind the bustling Cabin Bar where commotion will go unremarked. To make the act less murderous, he invites Judson to draw his own knife, and he plans to return to base when it is over, as if nothing has happened. But Prewitt sustains a long gash in his side and must hide out for the next six weeks to recuperate.

That Prewitt is never a suspect makes Judson's murder a middle-brow "lost Eden" subplot. Although Prewitt's absence is noted the next morning and Judson's death is on the news, no one mentions the possible connection. Apparently the two sailors leaving the bar with Judson as Prewitt accosted him did not come forward; nor were other patrons questioned by police. Aside from Warden and his roll-call orderly (who has chosen not to report Prewitt as AWOL), no one at Schofield seemed to deduce that someone who had been in the stockade and subjected to Judson's treatment might be moved to murder him.

This oversight serves two ends. One is to render the stockade chimerical and thus insubstantiate this worst abuse of power. Once outside its walls, soldiers who have been there never talk of it; therefore, Judson in effect does not exist outside of the stockade. He himself asks Prewitt as he lies dying "Why'd you want to kill me?" (642). The war with Judson is a private one, a folkloric slay-the-evil-dragon plot for which Prewitt need not be blamed. The murder may not change the system, but it offers Prewitt a "separate peace."

Secondly, Prewitt's reprieve is also a test. He has a chance here to literally get away with murder—if he uses his head and acts in the interest of self-preservation. He does use his head in finally making contact with Warden, who has already entered the dragon-slaying plot by overlooking the AWOL for one week. Again, Warden seems to be the only soldier able to see through the "bolshevism" and accept Prewitt's devotion to the army as real.[7] Six weeks later, at the Blue Chancre bar, he counsels Prewitt that he has not been connected with the Judson murder, and he'd get nothing more than a one-month sentence for desertion if he returned immediately.

With some credible prescience, Prewitt refuses any plan that guarantees time in the stockade. His only other hope for a safe return to the military at this time (November 30, 1941), Warden advises, is to wait for the possible attack on Pearl Harbor and take advantage of the resulting confusion to reestablish himself with his company.

Warden thus demonstrates that the system can bend to accommodate Prewitt's temperament and values, and the coincidence of the Pearl Harbor attack makes the world a not entirely hostile environment for Robert E. Lee Prewitt. That Prewitt neglects the option, in fact stays drunk for eight days after the attack and makes himself easy pickings for MPs who are getting things back in order, unmistakably marks Prewitt as self-destructive. Prewitt's decision to return to base in late evening, after curfew, in military uniform is nothing short of suicide. He is shot as he crosses a golf course to evade the MPs, and he falls to death in a sandtrap.

The sandtrap scene, as a metaphorical indictment of the privileged system that Prewitt has withdrawn from, jeopardizes the argument that Jones is presenting Prewitt as loser more than victim. But the *more* is crucial. The middlebrow novel makes clear that, since imperfect systems victimize everyone, the smart thing to do is learn to compromise in order to survive them.

Warden is the one who accepts that in this world no one gets "the girl, the gold watch, and everything,"[8] and he is clearly the best army man of the novel. Significantly, he is a non-commissioned officer who refuses a commission that is his for the taking. Warden makes himself indispensable by running an organized, problem-solving, well-disciplined unit and thus can stand up to his superiors when he can't stomach their orders. He tells the newly arrived Prewitt: "Holmes is the CO, but he is like the rest of the officer class: a dumb bastard that signs papers an rides horses. . . . I'm the guy that runs this compny" (53).

Warden anticipates where his personal requirements and those of the army will tangle and avoids such junctures. He earns enough salary to maintain a pretty flush life style and attract women (he frequently boasts that "When I have to pay for it, I'll quit"). His reputation provides him some important control; for example, the means to slip Prewitt back into the company if the opportunity arises and the power to override a guard's orders to keep the ammunition depot locked.

For all his resentment of the army, Warden reveals during the Pearl Harbor attack that combat relieves some frustrations of a soldier's life: "Warden lowered his BAR, his belly and throat tightening with a desire to let loose a high hoarse senseless yell of pure glee. This is my outfit. These are my boys" (716-17). Jones describes the fighting in terms of sport: "The cooks had served them coffee and sandwiches. It had all been a sort of super-range-season with live targets to shoot at. The most exciting kind: Men" (724-25).

To view Warden as a role model is to underscore the theme that the successful man recognizes the limitations of the system, accepts what he can't change, and works with and around them. Shooting big weapons at vulnerable men is one socially acceptable means of venting frustration; getting drunk is another that is constantly and pointedly a part of the novel;[9] organized sports is another; sex is another.

Warden's use of sex for revenge is another middlebrow marker, for *using* a woman prevents his being the ideal role model in the folkloric, lowbrow sense, as does his inability in the highbrow sense to fully accept *why* he has used Captain Holmes's wife, Karen. The epitome of Slater's authoritarian philosophy, Holmes has driven Karen to promiscuity and cynicism (she got "the clap" from him and feels justified in revenging the curative hysterectomy that makes her feel like a "gutted shell") and turned his son into a rank-pulling brat (121).

Warden first seduces Karen because he sees cuckolding her husband as compensation for his inferior position. Having a woman like her at his disposal also bolsters his fantasy that he's a man who doesn't have to "pay for it." When they fall in love, Warden vacillates between a commitment to the purity and redemptive power of love and a dispassionate awareness of love's self-serving attributes.

In the novel's final scene, we see her aboard the evacuation ship, watching the Hawaiian harbor recede and engaging in coy conversation with a handsome young lieutenant who promises to get assigned to her dinner table. Back at the Blue Chancre Bar, Warden is already fondling the thighs of a prostitute. Thus ends a love affair of such intensity that each thought of it as a probable high point of their lives. They turn immediately and without reflection to new sexual dalliance.

Such fickleness might give the lie to their romantic commitment or indicate highbrow cynicism, but either reading is offset by the "compensatory motif" of middlebrow fiction.[10] Warden had come to their final tryst afraid that confessing to Karen that he has torn up his commission and rejected his opportunity to become an officer will end their love. Warden is delighted by her reaction to the news: "You've known it all along? . . . and you still came anyway? . . . even when Holmes forbade you? . . . I'm a long way from worth it" (785).

Karen's desire to be with him in spite of his unimproved standing and her husband's orders to terminate her affair seems to be all Warden needs: the affirmation is as good as a wedding.[11]

And Karen has gotten something similar from Warden. When he protests that he has taken everything from this relationship, given nothing, she replies: " 'You've given me my freedom. Dana can never . . . hurt me any more. . . . You've made me loved' "(786). Having thus reassessed their own worth, these two can go on pretty much as they have done before they met, but with a new self-concept and a (middlebrow) compensatory memory that dull the pain inflicted by the "powers that be": Dana Holmes.

Warden's is really the only winning strategy of the novel: he knew his opponents, knew that siding with them would be his own annihilation, and settled for the best that he could manage: his own little bailiwick of authority and a piece of tail from the boss's wife. What he teaches Prewitt is that if you don't put up your fists and box you get wiped out.

In *From Here to Eternity*, characters have to learn to deal with situations which are determined not by universal features of humanity, but by features of a particular point in time. That viewpoint is essential to the novel's ambivalent implication that one should simultaneously pity Prewitt, Warden, and Karen Holmes for being outside the golden age of history, admire them for the independent stands they take against this misfortune, yet hold them accountable for not taking the full measure of what those conditions are and acting accordingly. Lee S. Halprin puts Jones in a large group of writers reluctant to give up on civilization's power to civilize who resort to the metaphor of " 'good men under the heel of institutional power.' "[12]

Middlebrow war novels, then, foreground the writers' misgivings about social institutions. What lowbrow war novels do instead is camouflage misgivings, by putting the enemies on the opposite side of the trenches or within the characters themselves. In a lowbrow battlefield, good is rewarded, proper behavior and attitude are teachable, and systems work. People who suffer or fail may sometimes be the victims of ill luck or poor timing, but more often have themselves to blame for not learning how to be a "real man" or a "real woman," for not doing what authority figures hold them responsible to do, for not giving of themselves, or for not trusting that things work according to supportive laws.

That is not to say that the realistic lowbrow war novel falsifies reality to the extent that no COs are sadistic bastards and America wages only morally justifiable war. The improprieties of the system may be acknowledged, but relegated to the shadowy doubling of possibilities, as Metalious used in *Peyton Place*.[13] When the boys in Leon Uris's *Battle Cry* talk about the lousy commander of a neighboring battalion, readers are thereby cautioned not to expect real life to work so systematically, but in effect encouraged to behave *as if* the world accorded justice.

The absent implication is that one doesn't make things any better by not playing by the rules, so you may as well go along with them and hope for the best. Herman Wouk turns what seems like a middlebrow novel into a standard lowbrow in order to make such a point. *The Caine Mutiny*, untypically for lowbrow fiction, features the pathological behavior of the CO, as well as the crew's resentment and fear of his power over their lives.

The rectitude of relieving Captain Queeg of his command seems confirmed when the court martial acquits Keith of mutiny. But that affirmation is undone by defense attorney Greenwald's parting shot to the author Keefer. Greenwald argues that if he wrote a war novel he'd make "a hero out of old Yellowstain" because he's the kind of grunt who's been "standing guard on this fat dumb and happy country of ours."[14] Lowbrow characters must follow a standard code—not their own logic.

In lowbrow war novels, historical truth plays a relatively unimportant part, despite the fact that realistic data about the daily life of combat soldiers accounts for much of their interest.[15] Edward Beach's *Run Silent, Run Deep* (1955), a lowbrow novel about the submarine corps, looks like the diary/logbook of an officer who started out with a group of green kids and watched them turn into an effective, monolithic fighting force.

The detailed account shows how greenhorns adapt to a war effort, but it also shows how men commit themselves to their officers and to each other. The selection of data in a lowbrow novel makes it clear that a soldier is not concerned with ultimate political or economic goals of war, nor with a chance for personal satisfaction, but with how best to do the job that is specifically his to do. Justifying, analyzing, or profiting from war is someone else's job.

This slant enables Uris to bypass typical fifties critique of military structure. Where middlebrow writers like Mailer, Jones, and Hersey suggest that the normative attributes of military leaders are arrogance, personal ambition, capriciousness, and indifference toward the welfare of their troops (sometimes verging on sadism), Uris operates with a naturalized "sense of social structure" wherein characters are *not* dehumanized by unsympathetic officers.[16] The icy detachment of Uris's officers ultimately proves effective in serving the warriors' most urgent needs.

Those who serve under Sixth Battalion Commander Major Huxley see him as a "hell of a good man" despite his brusqueness. Though he kept a sort of "arrogant distance from the enlisted men," they "couldn't help but respect him. No matter how he drove his men, you would always find old Highpockets at the head of the column."[17]

Military discipline rates automatic respect in this novel. When Huxley ignores that and confronts General Pritchard because he disagrees with this officer's decision on how to use his regiment, Pritchard reacts like one of Jones's officers: "No blood-hungry Marine is going to tell me how to run my campaign. . ." (229). Several months later, when Sixth Regiment has again drawn a secondary assignment, Huxley commits the same breach of conduct, and he receives a similar tongue-lashing from General Snipes.

The difference between Jones's or Mailer's officers and Uris's is that Huxley gets listened to instead of court-martialed. Although Pritchard overrules his request for a more significant role in the battle, he lets Huxley go without reprimand. Snipes makes the improbable turnaround, gives Huxley the dangerous duty that he came after, and ends the interview with "a slight smile on his lips" and his face looking "warm and human" (450).

Neither Snipes's smile nor Huxley's anxiety for his men to get more dangerous assignments is to be taken as sadistic. While Huxley obviously doesn't care for his men on a personal basis, he believes in giving them the chance they deserve to prove themselves as real men, does his level best to train them to handle the worst, and undergoes exactly the same rigors and risks as his troops. Besides, his squad sergeants fulfill soldiers' needs for personal concern. In this case the novel's narrator, "Mac," acts as something of a housemother, available for heart-to-heart talks when any of "his boys" needs counseling on how to get their heads on straight or tie up with the right woman.

The military establishment in *Battle Cry* treats its soldiers well, gives them conscientious training, right-headed leaders, good equipment, and plenty of leave time to keep their spirits up and forge romantic alliances. Mac and Huxley are in effect the good parents who give their boys support and put them through their proper paces. As "father," Huxley knows that without undertaking the ultimate challenge of facing death, one is forever lost in self-centeredness. A *good* leader like Huxley believes that facing a challenge will make his men both proud and free. Not death or even particular bravery, but the *willingness* to lose one's life for others earns a spot in Valhalla.

Joseph J. Waldmeir says that post-war novelists realized that idealistic themes didn't work unless soldiers *chose* to act. But choosing to kill is too evil; rebuffing enemy ideology too unrealistic. Responsibility to a leader and to a corps is a compromise solution.[18] The "battle cry" of "Huxley's Whores" is not for the fatherland, but for their brethren. They achieve their greatest spirit when, on the brink of collapse, the company is inspired to revenge Huxley's death in battle: "Huxley's Whores rose to the heights of their dead captain . . . [shrieking] 'Blood! BLOOD!' " (468).

As "mother," Mac oversees other important aspects of their maturation: how to keep a manly spirit and especially how to make appropriate love alliances. Though this "gung-ho" Marine yarn seems to spend too much time on romantic liaisons, they're clearly part of folkloric character-building. Marriage takes up more of a man's life than warfare, so it's logical that a "how-to-become-a-man" yarn has more pairing up than paring up. Edward Beach's, *Run Silent, Run Deep*, focuses on Jim Bledsoe's need to learn to swallow authority before he is man enough to wield it. His growth towards responsible leadership parallels his evolution from cocky, detached husband to solid, committed one.

Much of *Battle Cry* shows how various individuals overcome unsureness or ineptitude to achieve fulfilling heterosexual pairings. For example, the main character, eighteen-year-old Danny Forrester, all-American football player adored by his high school sweetheart Kathy, can't decide to commit himself to her. He is more or less seduced by the wife of an absent corporal and forgets Kathy, his family, military responsibility, and all erstwhile moral standards to carry on an ardent affair.

Finally realizing that Kathy is his true love, he wonders how he could have gotten so tangled with Elaine. An older, married GI explains: "Elaine Yarborough is like a million wives. She's lived in . . . a circle of boredom . . . she wants to escape. Just an age-old frustration, Danny'" (95-6). Never mind the indictment against virtually all modern marriage; this analysis suffices for Danny. On his next furlough, he marries Kathy, never gives Elaine a second thought, and goes on to become the perfect soldier.

Mac counsels Marion Hotchkiss (called "Sister Mary" because of his asceticism and mild ways) to go ahead and marry the woman he loves even after he discovers that she's a prostitute. Mac gets Hotchkiss to admit that nothing really matters except how important Rae is to him, and then he, too, is ready to be a good soldier.

Andy Hookans, a big Swede who's never been very successful with women, has several lessons to learn. Andy reacts with comments like "Them dirty no good bitches!" to news that someone has been jilted (145). When Pat Rogers, a lively, attractive young widow, warms up to him, he nearly loses her by blurting out that she must be hard up for a lay.

Later when he finds another man at her apartment, he gets angry a second too quickly—just before the guy introduces himself as Pat's cousin. She finally has to throw herself at Andy to convince him that she loves him. Then the love becomes so overwhelming to him that he wants to desert rather than lose it. He is "saved" only after he realizes that "sometimes there is something more important than just two people" (372-73) and decides to return to his company.

Constantine Zvonski errs on the other end of the trust scale. Without consulting his fiancée, he takes on dangerous and lucrative extra duty and saves every dime he can make at boot camp to finance her trip to San Diego so that they can marry. Predictably he is devastated by her "Dear John" letter and eventually makes a suicidal one-man stand against the enemy which enables his buddies to escape and assures his death.

Knowing how to negotiate the challenges of courtship seems to require listening to your heart, but also keeping your ears open and seeking others' advice. Connie fails apparently because he isolates himself, doesn't confide in his elders, and really doesn't listen to Susie: he trusts himself and serves himself. Contrasting his failure to others' successes suggests that life's satisfaction requires the submergence of self, primarily into a heterosexual relationship, secondarily into a tribe, thirdly into the State.

Like the lowbrow novel, the highbrow war novel operates on a sense of absolute faith, but here it's an inverse faith that institutions are corrupt, that the asylum is run by the inmates, and that humans are by nature more grasping than gracious. In the highbrow novel, there is no sense of morally correct and incorrect behavior; there is faith instead in the indifference of the universe and the innate indifference of humans to other humans on whom they do not depend.

While *Battle Cry* suggests that allegiances virtually guarantee satisfaction, John Hawkes's highbrow novel, *The Cannibal*,[19] guarantees the opposite. In Hawkes's world, allegiance merely justifies acts of self-serving or self-satisfying violence. The submergence of self, lack of self awareness, the resurgence of systems of allegiance to leaders or nations only perpetuate patterns of victimization that amount to cannibalism.[20] Greiner sees "territorial imperative" as a controlling influence where death is less important than "the piling of bricks, the desperate attempts of the tenant" (155). Rovit says Hawkes throws "pious patterns" into derangement and negates "godly" notions of justice, mercy, and order.[21] Eat or be eaten.

The Cannibal takes place at the end of World War II in a small city in Germany which has been devastated by aerial bombing, depletion of men and materials, the occupation by American troops, and the widespread disorder of a defeated, impoverished nation. Rioting inmates have fled from the insane asylum. Corpses clog the city's canal and pollute its water supply. With nearly all civilizing struts removed, characters act out their personal scenarios of self-preservation.

Zizendorf, the egotistical narrator, plots the assassination of Leevey, the American overseer of this occupied district, in order to take control himself. The women in the novel are equally tactical. Jutta, Zizendorf's daily sex partner, whom he believes loves him "without sense," has apparently become a prostitute to keep herself going until she hears something of her husband, who was on the Russian front. Her older sister, Stella Snow, has turned their family mansion into a boarding house. She "knew the strength of women, and sometimes vaguely hoped that a time would come again when they could attack flesh with their husbands' sickles" (173).

In the novel's most grotesque sequence Stella's boarder stalks Jutta's pubescent son, who is referred to only as "the fairy." In the penultimate scene the "Duke" catches the boy, drags him to the woods, and butchers him as a hunter might a rabbit or a fox.

The next morning he invites Stella to dine with him, declaring "I have been most fortunate, and the meal is now being prepared" (220). Stella is delighted with the invitation. No one, except the boy's younger sister, who knew that "little girls were safe because they were the ones who waited and never moved" (152), seems to have noted the Duke's quest (though it is mentioned ten times in the novel). No one worries when the boy is gone an entire night. This fact enhances the surrealism of the novel, for it almost seems that the Duke is a ghost or that the whole town is somnambulant.

The boy's capture, however, has been observed with perverse satisfaction by Stella's son. The Duke had cornered the boy in the empty theater (young Snow and his wife live upstairs). When Snow hears the cries of two womanly voices (one "like his mother's"), he drags himself out of bed, bumps his way down a flight of steps, and blithely accepts the Duke's explanation that he has come to retrieve the errant boy home. Snow returns upstairs, feeling "an uncommon pleasure in the visit of the Duke and the night's events" (189-90).

That pleasure translates into a determination to have sex with his wife—perhaps for the first time since he lost his leg ("Leg or no leg she'd lose [her pants] again"). Hawkes describes his voice when he wakens his wife as "high and unnatural"—like that of the Duke's in the scene he just witnessed (20).

The parallels emphasize Hawkes's method of depicting human motivation metonymically. The Duke, still seeing himself as the warrior/hunter, revenges his loss of power and status by preying upon something weaker than himself. He can still impress women with the spoils of conquest. Made impotent and immobile as a casualty of war, Snow identifies with the character of the Duke, who is here both the conqueror and his mother—the most potent character in the novel. The encounter renews his image of himself as stronger than his wife and reminds him that woman's lust will induce them to yield their pants.

In the context of a town devastated by "justified" depravity of war, such displaced aggression discharges the reader's justification for judging the Duke depraved, young Snow ghoulish, Zizendorf megalomaniacal, Jutta promiscuous, and so forth. In a world devoid of civilized and moral means of having an impact, being heard, or achieving well-being, the characters in *The Cannibal* make the most of what's available, behave in self-enhancing ways, and avoid despair. No one seems suicidal or terribly depressed.

Instead, many of the characters seem to fulfill Hawkes's aim that fiction should "revenge . . . the indignities of our childhood; it should be an act of rebellion against all the constraints of the conventional pedestrian mentality around us."[22] In the words of Ihab Hassan, Hawkes's characters repay outrage with outrage.[23]

Unlike the middlebrow motif of heeding the unique, this requital motif inscribes the repetitive nature of human behavior, human history, and human institutions. Hawkes's emphasis on place and time also enforces the broader concept of the universality of human behavior, the regularity of human events.

The setting of Germany proves especially useful because its history proceeds cyclically from 1870 in the Franco-Prussian War, to 1916-18 in World War I, to 1939-45 in World War II. Like Hawkes's characters, history copies another version of itself.[24] The book's division into three sections which double back on themselves (1945/1914/1945) shows how one era, one set of events both mirrors and engenders another. Albert Guerard says in the novel's introduction that Hawkes's history is "blind, inconsecutive, absurd. . ." (xi). As in *Oedipus* and in young Snow's imagination, it is a husband to its own mother.

The first section introduces Zizendorf's plan to murder Leevey.

The final section details the execution of Zizendorf's and the Duke's plots. The middle section shows Stella and Jutta as young girls and focuses especially on Stella's courtship and marriage to Ernie Snow, son of the owner of the beer hall where Stella had a brief career as a singer.

Their romance seems crucial to an understanding of Hawkes's themes, for Stella is given many dimensions in the novel. She is an eternal factor who "swept through ironclad centuries, a respected crone" (29). She is part Medea, part Circe, part Helen of Troy:

> Roasted apples fell from the bosom of an oracle, burnt and golden. . . . She covered the glass before her with the golden hair and saw for a moment in its swirling depths, the naked cowardice of [Ernie]. . . . and she laughed. . . . He was magnificent! (65)

Her attraction to Ernst is predatory, as suits the nature Zizendorf sees as hers: "The very hangman, the eater, the greatest leader of us all" (55). Ernie is attracted to her as a moth to a lamp. He runs after Stella and an English expatriate named Cromwell as their coach is departing from the beer hall: "He ran to spend energy, tried to run his own smallness into something large. . ." (73). Ernie's pursuit of Stella's carriage is made to replicate Gavrilo Princip's assassination of Archduke Ferdinand in Sarajevo:

> He ran up to them gasping. . . . Cromwell waited to see the short muzzle of the pistol . . . . But the carriage continued . . . and a crowd seemed to gather. . . . Francis Ferdinand lay on the seat of the carriage, his light shirt filled with blood . . . while the assassin, Gavrilo Princip, ran mad through the encircling streets. Obviously the advent of the great war would not throw them all together. . . . Ernie was ready, even in the throes of love . . . to fit into the conflict somewhere; and Stella knew only that she was climbing high and would someday lose him. . . . When the people found out . . . they caused a silent, spreading, impersonal commotion over the body of Ferdinand. (75)

The metaphoric love of a consuming woman for a man made to feel consummable parallels the behavior of nations ready to engage in war. The appetites of characters become the appetites of nations.[25] Hawkes's history, therefore, provides the warp to his characters' weft: History and character become inseparable in a way that makes Hawkes's historical sense something quite different from Uris's jingoism and

Jones's nostalgia. National characteristics and national history are factors which impel behavior. Stella's ancestors, Hawkes writes,

> had run berserk, cloaked themselves in animal skins, carved valorous battles on their shields. . . . Stella, with such a history running thickly in her veins, caught her breath and flung herself at the feet of her horned and helmeted kinsmen. . . . (61)

Those horns take on personal meaning when Ernst sees his father approach his death bed: "Old Snow . . . had horns . . . terrible, agonizing, deformed short stubs protruding from the wrinkled crown. . . . Hating the devilish return of boisterous heroic Herman, Ernst died. . ." (142).

Where a middlebrow novel would make scapegoats of Ernst (who died of flu shortly after his marriage to Stella) and Jutta's son, and use their deaths to mark ends and beginnings, they only mark recurrent cycles in Hawkes's novel—such as Stella's consumption of Germany, Ernst, and now her sister's son. O'Donnell points out that mythically the discharge of violent energy against a scapegoat dissipates that energy and purifies the community (as Prewitt's death does perhaps), but in *The Cannibal* it merely serves to keep the cycle going (21-37). War, rather than being the result of a momentary influence (the Archduke's assassination), emerges from the conflation of certain omnipresent conditions bound to erupt at periodic times and places.

This use of history denies that Hawkes's choice of setting is designed to moralize about atavistic German character and the probable rebirth of German belligerence.[26] Undoubtedly it is difficult for any of us living in the late twentieth century to forget the connections among Germany, Hitler, unmotivated aggression, antisemitism, and the "final solution" and believe that Hawkes's choice of Germany is unmotivated by offense at these issues. The spectres of German aggression and Jewish extermination haunt the book, but these spectres reflect Hawkes's images of the human soul in a post-modern world in general. They're the worst horror he had at hand to depict the depth of our alienation from each other.

More practical reasons for choosing the German setting are that his subject required a devastated town and that Hawkes's mid-century American audience was likely to know significant events of modern German history. Fifties readers would come equipped with some historical knowledge essential to filling out their "horizon of expectations."[27] Furthermore, the choice of a foreign country and a recent enemy serves Hawkes's desired effect of aesthetic distance. O'Donnell quotes Hawkes on the subject: "I knew that what I was writing was so emotionally charged . . . that only considerable detachment would make it possible to write fiction in the first place" (16).

Hawkes seems far less interested in the outrages of war, Nazism, Hitler, and the Holocaust than he is in the ways in which the common citizenry are swallowed up and spat out by personal and impersonal forces alike. He seems far more interested in demonstrating how individual behavior parallels that of the nation as a whole—a point that cannot be made without examining both the narrow and wide perspectives, without being both close and distant. The setting of Germany provides that distance; the familiarity of Germany's struggles provides some closeness; Hawkes's invention of Spitzen-on-Dein provides the microscope.

A war-torn world allows for examination of both personal and impersonal aggression, and the characters in Hawkes's novel illustrate various ways of dealing with aggressors. Jutta chooses the method that will leave her the most of herself; her daughter recognizes a truth and thus survives; the "fairy" runs, but is no match for the Duke's strength, determination, and rank. Men fare worse than women, for they must fight or flee; either method places them in greater jeopardy than women, who can offer distractions or control in non-threatening ways.

The survivors in this tale, particularly Stella and the Duke, are witty, instinctual, and unburdened by compassion or conscience. Thomas Armstrong implies all three of these characteristics in pointing out that the Duke, in asking his curious question to Jutta's son before abducting him in the movie theater ("Would you like to buy a ticket?"), has transformed himself into an actor following a script (832).

There is no room for sentimentality here, no yearning for an earlier era when officers were gentlemen, nor false highlighting of officers who are gentlemen. Hawkes portrays a world in which no one is gentle by nature, though some are by design, and all are either aggressors—cannibals—or prey. The aggressors find their pleasure in power and survival. The prey either succumb or adapt.

Though *The Cannibal* is, as Ihab Hassan asserts, "one of the deepest books to come out of World War II,"[28] it is a grim and difficult novel which gained no popular following[29] and only limited literary acclaim. Rowit says that *The Cannibal* is "life-affirming" because it's absurd and ironic, and it "enlarges the trivial" while it "diminishes the grandiose" (160). Opposite of lowbrow fiction, which countermands the grimness of life by insisting on the attainability of the grandiose, *The Cannibal* insists that we confront the grim if we are to avoid being swallowed by it.

Readers who love a book like *Battle Cry* better than the other two novels discussed in this chapter are those who, in Guerard's words, look for "consoling nineteenth century pleasures" (57). *Battle Cry* makes it clear enough that human dignity is hard to realize, for it requires not only that humans endure brutal tests and extreme sacrifices in order to achieve it, but also that they have a bit of luck in drawing a good hand—the right skipper, the right buddies, the most challenging opportunities. But the novel also emphasizes that people enhance their own fates by "doing the right thing" and being selfless. If that seems a little Sunday-schoolish, at least it guarantees more than middlebrow or highbrow novels the possibility of maintaining a sense of human dignity, whatever the particularities of present conditions.

What *From Here to Eternity* promises is at best a chance to cut your losses, along with a warning that you're bound to lose it all if you do try to hang on to outmoded notions of personal integrity. The "trivial" (petty-minded officers, personal slights, intractable systems, details of present and immediate history) is aired, but grievance is disallowed. Those who love this novel might do so because they regard themselves as unsentimental realists. They can see why the self-preserving instincts of the id have to be subjugated if social order is to survive.

Revealing highbrow's hypervaluation of the id, *The Cannibal* implies the importance of dealing with the trivial, of waging personal battle with a hostile environment. Armstrong says that Hawkes's readers are required to expend conscious effort to become aware (833); Greiner says they must participate in the creative process. The "compensatory motif" here is that you can wage that battle on your own terms; you're not bound to any norms of behavior (96) and you're not obliged—in fact, not invited—to see the world as others see it nor to trust that the information that world proffers is useful information.

What *The Cannibal* permits is the right to go for your own brass ring—before someone else gets to it. That compensation, as O'Donnell says is true of Hawkes's reconciliations, is temporary, dynamic, and open-ended (20). It is created and recreated out of the irony and absurdity of an enlarged triviality. Fans of *The Cannibal* may seem unsentimental or disillusioned, more willing to accept despair than to disgorge on hope. At the same time, they seem more interested in human behavior and human capacity than in abstract institutions or institutionalized abstractions, more interested in the id than in the superego.

NOTES

1. "Bricolage" is the term Claude Lévi-Strauss gives to this description of what tale-makers do. *The Savage Mind* (1962; London: Weidenfeld, 1966), 16-21.

2. All of these reasons come together in William Bradford Huie's account of a soldier executed for desertion at the end of WWII (*The Execution of Private Slovik*; New York: Dell, 1954). Private Slovik was an emotionally damaged young man, just on the verge of getting his life together, when he was drafted. He was so upset about having his chance for happiness snatched from him that he couldn't fight. Also interesting is that, though the book was published in 1954, the film and the paperback edition were not released until 1971, when the Vietnam Era made Slovik's sentiments much more socially acceptable.

3. James Jones, *From Here to Eternity* (New York: Signet, 1951), 328-30. Further page citations from this edition will be placed within the text. Jones's idiosyncrasies of style—the omission of the apostrophe in most contractions, the use of "compny" for "company," syntactical oddities, for example—will be preserved without comment. They are good examples of the self-conscious stylization that shows these to be characters in middlebrow rather than lowbrow novels.

4. Jerry H. Bryant sees the basic conflict of this book as a class struggle between the organization and the proletarian—an innately intelligent, heroically determined moral individual who seeks "no more than his due" from his corrupt "betters." *The Open Decision* (New York: Free, 1970), 120-21.

5. James R. Giles sees Prewitt as a highly idealistic fighter for the underdog who "opposes any institution acting corruptly or capriciously, even the beloved army when it is arbitrary or unfair." *James Jones* (Boston: Holt, 1981), 38-41.

6. Peter G. Jones argues that Prewitt punishes himself for breaking his vow of non-violence to his mother. *War and the Novelist* (Columbia: U of Missouri P, 1976), 33-34.

7. Giles explains that Prewitt personifies for Warden the emotion, passion, and artistic egotism that Warden denies in himself and thus metonymically unlocks him from his self-imposed role (51).

8. The title of a Travis McGee mystery by John D. MacDonald.

9. His defense lawyer argues that Prewitt should plead drunken indiscretion: "Nobody in the Army considers drunkenness . . . a sin. . . . Actually, most officers feel that a soldier who doesn't get drunked up and go on a rampage now and then . . . is a suspicious character" (492).

10. It's hard to know how much complexity to assign to Jones or his characters. Charles Rolo, in the March 1951 *Atlantic Monthly,* claims the book is much better than Mailer's for having "its own undoctored truth" and "magnificent" characterizations. But he hedges in the final paragraph by wondering if Jones is "another of those emotionally retarded he-men to whom toughness is the supreme Good" (83-4). Giles corroborates the criticism, labeling Jones's a "thor-

oughly commonplace mind . . . arrested in adolescence" like "that of Leon Uris and Harold Robbins" (32-3).

11. His elation supports Giles's opinion that the novel is "about an exploited class." Giles sees Warden as a person who hates the middle class—including the Holmeses—and his ability to win Karen over on his terms rather than hers as emblematic of Warden's "just deserts" (61).

12. "American Liberalism: Literature and World War II," *Minnesota Review* 3 (Winter 1963): 179. Peter Jones accounts for the ambivalence by calling the book a *bildungsroman* in which Prewitt's "passage into manhood is impossible, his initiative fatal" (32). Frederich R. Karl says that Jones never shows how Prewitt's struggle can make sense when he has volunteered for an organization which punishes individuality. *American Fiction 1945-1980: A Comprehensive History and Critical Evaluation* (New York: Harper, 1983), 102.

13. See chapter one.

14. Herman Wouk, *The Caine Mutiny* (1951; New York: Pocket, 1973), 571-2.

15. Carmichael says the "painstaking documentation" assures readers that these books are true, but laments that readers thereby grow "knowledge-proud" on such trivialization. Rev. of *Exodus*, *Midstream* (Autumn 1961), 87-9.

Edward Weeks praises the "big job" *Battle Cry* does. "Young Marines," *Atlantic Monthly* (August 1953), 84.

Paul V. Farrell says Uris's skill at "straight reporting" yields a "somewhat corny but strangely exhilarating yarn." "U.S. Marines," Rev. of *Battle Cry* in *Commonweal* (8 May 1953), 129.

16. Miller, 149.

17. Leon Uris, *Battle Cry* (New York: Bantam, 1953), 4. Further citations will be indicated in the text; idiosyncrasies of the author's style are preserved without comment.

18. *American Novels of the Second World War* (The Hague: Mouton, 1969), 140-42.

19. (New York: J.J. Little and Ives, 1949). Quotations will be cited from this edition.

20. Donald J. Greiner, *Comic Terror: The Novels of John Hawkes* (Memphis: Memphis State UP, 1975), 74-75.

21. Earl Rovit, "The Fiction of John Hawkes: An Introductory View," *Modern Fiction Studies* 11.2 (1964): 161-2.

Webster Schott sees the existentialism as fatalistic, speaking of human decline, failure and collapse, the universal triumph of evil. "Vision of a Nightmare," *Nation* (2 Sept 1961), 122-3.

22. Frederick Busch, *Hawkes: A Guide to his Fictions* (Syracuse: Syracuse UP, 1973), xv.

23. "The Novels of Outrage: A Minority Voice in Postwar American Fiction," *American Scholar* 34 (September 1965): 241.

24. Greiner says that history is like a character in this novel (68).

25. For further discussion see Thomas W. Armstrong, "Readers, Critics and the Form of John Hawkes's *The Cannibal*," *Boundary 2* 5 (1977): 835-36, and Patrick O'Donnell, *John Hawkes* (Boston: Holt, 1982), 39.

26. Though Greiner reads the novel as a warning about the resurgence of German aggression (85), he says Hawkes uses Germany as a setting because our distance from it lessens fears we would harbor about ourselves (242). Busch argues that Hawkes wants Zizendorf to sound "the voice of Germany," which speaks with "sardonic ease" about murder (36).

27. The term is Hans Robert Jauss's from *Toward an Aesthetic of Reception*, trans. Timothy Bahti, Theory and History of Literature 2 (Minneapolis, U of Minnesota P, 1982), 18-45.

28. "The Dismemberment of Orpheus: Reflections on Modern Culture, Language, and Literature," *American Scholar* 32 (1963): 478.

29. Alexander Klein says the novel "makes dullness and surrealism practically synonymous." "The Merely New," *New Republic* (27 March 1950), 20.

Bruce Bawer calls it "incoherent." *Diminishing Fictions: Essays on the Modern American Novel and Its Critics* (St. Paul, MN: Graywolf, 1988), 221.

Wallace Markfield calls Hawkes's a "diffuse, uncontrollable talent." "Three First Novels," *Commentary* (April 1950), 392.

VI

THE DIVIDED SELF[1]

Morris Dickstein calls the novel a "child of the marketplace,"[2] the offspring of a self divided between the individualist opportunities provided by capitalism and empiricism and the social inclinations toward the security of home and the status quo. Every novel struggles with this rift, and the conformist fifties provide an especially apt theater of the human spirit torn between the desires of the inner self for a sense of home and community and of the outer self for a piece of the pie.

Restoring a unity is the aim of every novel, as indicated by Roland Barthes' assertion that all plots "lead to the Oedipus": humans struggle to return to the source of succor after being set adrift from the haven of the hearth.[3] Michele Roberts implies the lowbrow method of recuperation in her suggestion that the heroine's capitulation to the hero's wooing is a return to the "blissful breast" or to the kind of succor that a mother gives.[4] Barthes explains how reading itself enables highbrow recovery when writing refuses to be taken as a representation of reality. The highbrow text "desires the reader" to aim for the "third meaning," which is neither represented reality nor inner self-fulfillment, but a meaning that is negotiated in the passage between language and significance.[5] The similarity between lowbrow and highbrow recovery will be discussed in chapter seven.

The recovery process of the middlebrow novel is akin to Claude Lévi-Strauss's explanation of "myth-work." Lévi-Strauss says that every myth resolves a contradiction of a social reality, mediating the "raw" and the "cooked" or things as they are found in nature and things as they are reordered by civilization. For example, the need to mate is a natural, instinctual, or "raw" factor of human intercourse; the appropriateness of a particular mate is culturally determined or "cooked." It is the job of myth to make what is "cooked" appear to be natural, so that the restraints (taboos) a culture imposes on natural inclinations (to mate with a family member, for example) appear to serve natural instincts while they in fact serve broader aims of the community.[6]

In Lukács's words, the novel is the epic of a "world that has been abandoned by God";[7] its ontology is empiricist, its discipline capitalist, its rewards materialist. It precludes miraculous, improbable, or idealized solutions and allows only reasonable, practicable, and external ones. The world view of the "true novel" differs from lowbrow and highbrow novels, which derive their recuperation from the order of abstract law rather than the order of society. In lowbrow and highbrow novels repressed urges reunite in ways ordained by "God." But because the order of God no longer coincides with Cartesian social order, one must reach outside the social order for reunification—through wish-fulfillment, imagination, or language itself.

The middlebrow novel eschews that reach, disdains the power of the imagination, and exalts the power of reality to satisfy individual needs, acknowledging the loss with a consolation prize instead of reunification. Middlebrow novels do not deny the divided self, but they suggest that the repressed is preserved only in the private realm and accessible only in glimpses. What goes on in observable life, in the here and now, *in time*, is what characters must attend to.

Lukács says that in the novel meaning separates from life and the essential from the temporal: time replaces God as the essence of things. The social, the institutional, and the civilized are repressive as well as immutable; only our way of dealing with them is variable (121-23). Every middlebrow novel has a similar message: If you wish to succeed in the outside world, you must do so on its terms; if you wish to achieve what your soul craves, you must nurture and protect it in memory and in privacy or lose the rewards the world has to offer.[8]

Since we *have* lost the epic certainty that what is cooked is really raw, recuperation of the social and inner self is a confidence game in the middlebrow novel. With no divine fiat, no master design, no subconsciously imbedded plot elements, the middlebrow novelist must *contrive reasons* for things to occur as they do and to imply that what happens to the protagonist is likely to happen to an average person. The need for contrivance makes the middlebrow novel more vulnerable to mistakes than highbrow or lowbrow. It's easier to see their plots and characters as constructs.

For example, in order for readers to accept that Tom Rath is able to keep his job at United Broadcast Corporation after declaring that he doesn't care to work as hard as Hopkins wants him to, Wilson must rationalize Hopkins' desire to make a son out of Rath. To this end, Hopkins' own father is depicted as a detached bully; Hopkins,in turn, has lost his own son by bullying him into the army. The subplots involving the sneaky servant, the neurotic father, the profligate grandmother, the responsible war buddy, and the judicious judge create force fields that determine certain outcomes: All help to manufacture whatever credibility there is in this protagonist's success and the limits of that success.

The "happy" middlebrow ending posits that exterior goals can be satisfied without entirely sacrificing internal needs. Such endings work if whatever makes external life manageable for the protagonist is not unduly fortuitous or unlikely and whatever keeps the inner self alive is somehow adequate. *The Man in the Gray Flannel Suit* comes close to the acceptable compromise. Though Tom will have a satisfactory private life—a nice house with a beautiful view, a nice, pretty wife, a reawakened sex life, and nice healthy kids—his only connections to the yearnings of his soul are memories of the idyllic affair with his Italian lover and the wartime experience.

The Man in the Gray Flannel Suit does not satisfy entirely because it's too easy to detect the contrivance.[9] The rekindling passion between Tom and Betsy represents one of the "big lies" of the fifties and sixties: salvation through sexual liberation. Sexuality may be one of the few channels of spirited self-expression available to modern society (or a way of reclaiming the "things of the body" from their negative Cartesian image).

John P. Sisk says that too much attention to sex is a sign of political and social despair; political powerlessness often throws an impossible burden on sex and/or transfers disillusions to it.[10] Fisk's view implies that the consolation prize is a concocted mediator, and it supports Barthes's criticism that popular culture myths eradicate history and render changes in the social order harmless.[11] Joseph Waldmeir concurs that "novels of 'accommodation' blunt the social critical impulses of the fifties."[12] Still, if accommodation is recognizable as such and is not particularly comfortable accommodation, at least some social criticism remains in place.

But, more importantly, what's lacking in Wilson's book, as well as in Helen Howe's *Circle of the Day*, is a believable struggle toward that consolation prize. Faith Millet merely listens to a few opinions about marital infidelity and takes a more careful reading of the relationships in her life before she decides to stay with the husband who has been unfaithful to her. The fact that she never cries or lashes out makes her something of a cipher in this drama, a *function* of social situations rather than a master of them. The easy capitulation is dissatisfying.[13]

She and Tom Rath are deflated in the same way as some of Sinclair Lewis's characters and perhaps Joseph Heller's in his novels after *Catch-22*: by having wishes confined to the size of their surroundings.[14] Where Yossarian's anxiety at risking his life to follow nonsensical orders of nonexistent superiors bespeaks a deep and extensive agony, Bob Slocum's vague dissettlement that "something happened" doesn't substantiate his pain.

The *acknowledgment* of the pain seems more important in what makes a middlebrow novel work than does the salve applied to the ache. Because problems are foreordained as insoluble, middlebrow novels serve their functions by merely recognizing the pain and its sources. Bettelheim describes a system of Hindu medicine in which patients find and contemplate their own stories—a process which discloses unconscious conflicts and makes explicit and acceptable the sources of the pain. When patients understand what troubles them, they get better (25). In Bettelheim's words, "Anxiety faced is anxiety mastered" (127).

The sources of the pain are what cause middlebrow novels to differ from era to era. We can look back to the muckraking novels from the early part of the century and see that management's brutal treatment of labor was one spur of classic middlebrow fiction—such as Upton Sinclair's *The Jungle*. The indignities of the Depression spawned classic works from Steinbeck and Erskine Caldwell. After the rebellious sixties, the theme of alien culture takes over, manifesting itself in a spate of spy novels (Forsyth, LeCarré) and novels in which protagonists—average person just doing their jobs—seem targeted for "punishment" without due cause and due process, as in Cheever's *Falconer*.

Showing that one *cooperates under duress* and pays a high price for the right to remain in the race is the middlebrow theme of Styron's novella, *The Long March*. Its hero, Mannix, an embittered Marine reserve called up to fight in Korea, stubbornly hikes thirty-six miles with a spike protruding into his boot, to prevent his superior from singling him out as a troublemaker. His badge of courage comes from a cleaning lady as he stumbles his way to the shower room:

> His ankle was the size of a grapefruit, an ugly blue, and this leg he dragged behind him. . . . Just then one of the Negro maids . . .

stopped, seeing Mannix, and said, "Oh my. . . . Do it hurt? . . . Oh, I bet it does. Deed it does." Mannix looked across the short yards that separated them. . . . The towel slipped away slowly from [his] waist and fell with a soft plop to the floor; Mannix . . . stood there . . . and blinked and sent toward the woman, finally, a sour, apologetic smile, his words uttered . . . not with self-pity but only with the tone of a man who, having endured and lasted, was too weary to tell her anything but what was true. "Deed it does," he said.[15]

James Jones's *From Here to Eternity* works on the inverse principle, of a hero who immolates himself by refusing to accept the privatization of the instinctual. Prewitt's insistence on pursuing self-expression, sexual satisfaction, and redress (in killing S/Sgt. Judson) guarantees that he can't thrive within the system. Yet it also assures his pervasive appeal to multitudes who enjoy reading about someone rejecting the system. Like the work of Dreiser and Steinbeck and the popular sixties protests, such as *One Flew Over the Cuckoo's Nest*, Jones's novel may satisfy those who see happiness as determined by the "adequacy of the deeds to the inner soul's demand for greatness."[16]

One of the most enduringly popular characters of fifties middlebrow fiction is Holden Caulfield, for Salinger has created an icon of the soul which wants the world to own up to its brutality.[17] Holden's experience has taught him that people of sensitivity, artistry, and fun don't survive in the adult world. Allie, the "nicest, most intelligent" brother, died as a teen; Holden's other brother, D.B., a poet, became a "prostitute" by writing Hollywood scripts; his parents are status seekers; most of the teachers he encounters at his various prep schools are "gameplayers." They're all phonies. They court meaningless success at the expense of meaningful relationships.

In his aim to be a "catcher in the rye," Holden reveals a number of desires: to be the kind of nurturing, protective parent he wanted but didn't get, to endure in natural surroundings, to do something important for others, to enjoy others' joy. Symbolically, Holden is also expressing ambivalent feelings about sexual maturity. Since the rye is where one body may meet another, to catch little ones before their great cataclysm virginalizes them; yet it's also a place where Holden may meet and tumble with another body.

Holden's obsession with Phoebe's childhood is not so much an effort to restore his own (as Humbert Humbert's is) but to salvage a piece of life that is still salvageable, to make it a *place* where people exist to calm and caress each other rather than to shape them up or ship them out. Jonathan Baumbach says that "to prevent 'the fall' is the only action to take against corruption."[18] Preventing the fall seems to be Holden's way of restoring the "lost Eden" that modern life has obliterated, by arresting the passage of time that makes our notions of happy camaraderie seem foolish. His happiest moment occurs while watching Phoebe's time-stopping ride on the carousel in Central Park: "I felt so damn happy . . . the way Phoebe kept going around and around" (213).

Like all middlebrow protagonists, Holden is plagued by the power of time to rob life of its essence. He worries about the schoolgirls he watches in the Biltmore lobby: "You kept wondering what the hell would happen to all of them. . . . You figured most of them would probably marry dopey guys. . ." (123). He shies away from personal relationships because he realizes that the forward motion of life leads to a falling away and because you can't miss what you've never had. At the novel's end Holden wistfully regrets sharing his story with others: "If you [tell anybody anything], you start missing everybody" (214).

This rueful revelation also illuminates another scene. Holden, kicked out of Pencey, calls a former teacher and accepts his offer of overnight lodging. The teacher, Antolini, is a good listener, and Holden reveals a good deal to him about what has gone wrong with his life. Later, sleeping on Antolini's couch, he awakens to find the man stroking his head. Holden jumps up, concocts a preposterous reason for leaving, and spends the rest of the night on a bench in Grand Central Station, horrified that he has been the target of a homosexual pass.

The incident reiterates Holden's intense fear of human relationships: Once you start caring about someone you miss them; what once was good goes away. Holden admits that Antolini is a good guy; he remembers him as the only faculty member to approach the body of the boy who flung himself from the school windows, and the one who took off his suitcoat to wrap the bloody corpse. To be "fathered" by this man—which Holden reflects later is a reasonable explanation of the head stroking—is to weaken his resolve to trust no one: Care about him and he'll disappear like Allie.

The protagonist of such a story has to be an immature adolescent, for no one would believe such raw emotion in an adult.[19] Adults must defend themselves against the desires Holden has and do what Professor Spencer has told Holden he must do: learn to "play the game."

Nevertheless, Holden's story reflects the widespread frustration of readers who long for legitimate work to do, for freedom to act naturally and speak truthfully, for a concept of "normal" behavior that is not "a submission to totalitarian madness."[20] As Scheman points out, if you don't heed the writing on the wall (which in this book says "Fuck you"), you're designated crazy (76).

In creating this arguably masterful novel, Salinger avoids two common pitfalls of middlebrow writing. The first is the attempt to be too specific. Having to select a realistic grid whereon "true life" is played drives many a writer to do the job of a journalist—a job destined to failure.[21] Besides the fact that the chosen set of circumstances is bound to represent the reality of only a small segment of the readership, Goodman points out that there is no such thing as maximum specificity and maximum generality at the same time (56). The aim of many fiction writers to get the audience to say, "Yes, this is what it's really like," requires generalized rather than particular truth.

Salinger avoids the trap of particularity by attending to Holden's interchanges with characters instead of developing the fictionalized biographies that encumber novels like *The Man in the Gray Flannel Suit, Ten North Frederick,* and *The Group.* In other words, he follows Percy Lubbock's creative writing dictum of "show don't tell." Holden as schoolboy on the threshold of adulthood plays a role we all play: learning to assimilate what "any rational person" would or would not say or do. *Catcher in the Rye* was representative enough in the fifties to attract a vast and varied audience, perhaps because many people were moving into white-collar jobs where "businessspeak" and "businessdress" required more self-editing and self-mastery than did blue-collar employment of previous generations.

Another trap for middlebrow writers, basing the story on a dogmatic premise, overlaps with the representational one, for objective selection of detail is jeopardized if an author desires to portray a predetermined "truth." Salinger avoids dogmatism with subtlety and ambivalence. Whether it's "good" or "bad" that Holden will return to another prep school is dismissed in Holden's closing comments:

> "This one psychoanalyst guy . . . keeps asking me if I'm going to apply myself when I go back to school. . . . It's such a stupid question. . . . I mean how do you know what you're going to do till you *do* it?" (213)

His convalescence gives Holden time to reconsider his past and recover some positive memories of adults who were not phonies. Besides Antolini, there's Mr. Spencer, the Pencey history instructor who at least played straight and didn't preach, the nuns he talks to in the New York coffeeshop who are genuinely interested in his opinions about the characters in *Romeo and Juliet*, and D.B. His parents remain with the nagging "rest of them," while D.B. redeems himself by asking Holden what he thinks about things and listening to his answers. That Holden ends up in a psychiatric ward is also Foucauldian ambiguity: Who's wrong here, society or Holden?[22] The key to Holden's adjustment lies in seeking out those souls whose expansiveness matches his own—an effort that the reader can't know will happen until Holden "does it." This ending evades both recuperation and despair, while providing the possibility for either.

Such legerdemain is not found in McCarthy's *The Group*, for her world lacks ambivalence. None of her female characters is happy in marriage or out of marriage; no males know how to be decent husbands. McCarthy's world of marriage equals Wilson's world of business. Like that novel *The Group* gained a fair share of enthusiastic readers, probably because dogmatism looks like "telling it like it is" if you share the belief. Readers who have already given up hope are less likely to carp that nobody in McCarthy's novel lives happily ever after or happily at all and may relish hearing another voice say that. McCarthy depends on satire's ability to make the "cooked" seem "raw," yet thereby sacrifices resonance beyond the immediate taste environment.[23]

Granted, one can complain that readers of *Catcher in the Rye* must see a world full of phonies to accept Salinger's basic premise. But where Salinger provides at least some peripheral survivors of the system, McCarthy sees all as slain. Her overzealous indictments distort both generalness and genuineness and prevent us from mourning the victims.

McCarthy eschews standard novelistic techniques of suspense and character identification, and instead she depends heavily on shock value or sensationalism to engage readers' curiosity. *The Group* becomes a set of case studies of unhappy women, not unlike Betty Friedan's *The Feminine Mystique*, which set out to explain the "strange, stirring . . . sense of dissatisfaction" among American women.[24]

By being less novelistic, McCarthy's satire reaches for a different kind of recuperation than the two typically open to middlebrow novels: informed cooperation (Tom Rath) or martyrish rebellion (Prewitt). Because their vision has been narrowed by Vassar training and the

American concept of womanhood, McCarthy's characters can't see "the writing on the wall," but readers see their mistakes and their accommodations and are thus encouraged to feel superior to women who are probably their social superiors.

The character Polly Andrews, for example, described as having "a capacity for making lackluster friends,"[25] welcomes Gus LeRoy into her life after he's left a wife who's having an affair. Polly cooks for him, sleeps with him, accepts his explanations of why the divorce is delayed, and dreams of a blissful future as the second Mrs. LeRoy. The reader can see what's coming, though Polly doesn't. When he returns to his wife, Polly perpetuates her role as designated doormat by inviting her melancholic father to live with her. Passivity consigns her to a life of servility.

Another character who plays out women's-magazine roles is Libby, a twenty-four-year old virgin who expects that Mr. Right won't press for sex before marriage. When he appears as a Norwegian playboy ski instructor, she responds to his sexual advances with juvenile horror. She tries to knee him in the groin, and he shoves her into a bewildered heap, mocking "Oh what a bore you are, Elizabeth!" (235).

McCarthy's group all make mistakes of perception or self-assertion which diminish their stature in readers' eyes, and the objective omniscient narration furthers our detachment. Her "moral clarity comes at the expense of narrowing sympathies."[26] McCarthy even makes it hard to sympathize with the main character, Kay Leiland Strong, who is driven to suicide after her husband commits her to a mental institution in order to carry on an affair. The narrative renders this just deserts for a woman who took up every chic thing with a vengeance, married because it was chic, and then tried to mold her eccentric husband into a bourgeois *gentilhomme*.[27] The only character extended any admiration is Lakey, the expatriate lesbian who seems to know that America is not a place where one can be different and survive.

Though one might argue that McCarthy is creating a stronger sense of social critique, there is something carnivalesque in this parade of puppet princesses. Providing readers with a sense of superiority reverses disorder rather than recovers any kind of balance between inner and outer needs. More humor might have restored our sense of oneness with the characters. What also might have helped is something to ambiguate McCarthy's apparent conviction of who's right, such as Swift provides in the Houyhnhnm section of *Gulliver's Travels* or Heller does through Yossarian's instability.

McCarthy's novel may also fail to satisfy because she abandoned her original plan to extend the account over forty years. Except for Kay's story, the group members are glimpsed in static vignettes. Without the passing of time, these characters have inadequate opportunity to recognize culpability for their own suffering.

Recognizing the complicity facilitates a kind of compromise between the demands of the inner and outer worlds that takes the place of reclamation in such middlebrow novels as John O'Hara's *Ten North Frederick*. O'Hara's protagonist, Joseph Chapin, is as benighted as McCarthy's characters and similarly distanced from the reader by omniscient narration,[28] yet the passage of time enables him to recover a sense of self lost by his entry into a privileged social order.

"Ten North Frederick" is Joseph's birthplace in Gibbsville, Pennsylvania, and an emblem of the stature of its inhabitants—at least it was in an earlier era when birth and bearing were all a man needed to command respect. Buoyed by this bogus birthright, Joe aspires to high political office. As with McCarthy's Vassar grads, his sense of immunity leads him to fatal mistakes: he doesn't learn party protocol; he offends Mike Slattery, the local party boss; he's unwilling to start in a lowly position.

But *time* provides the lesson; years of waiting for the "call" ready him for the *coup de grâce*. When he appears before a nominating board, having expressed his desire to be lieutenant governor and given Slattery forty thousand dollars to favor his candidacy, he is told that the party "can't affort to gamble on a man who is not a proven vote-getter." He withdraws with swift grace and goes on a three-day drunk.[29]

Ten North Frederick ends with Chapin's love affair with his daughter's roommate, Kate Drummond, a "cool, self-sufficient beauty" (368). O'Hara does not explain the attraction they have for each other, though he emphasizes its depth. Especially given that it begins after Chapin has become a despondent man heavily into drink, it is as unrealistic a turn as Maria's romance with Tom Rath or Prewitt's unnoted assassination of S/Sgt. Judson.

This affair is short-lived and Chapin soon dies of a liver ailment. But the relationship does provide readers an antidote to despair. An unhappy middlebrow ending usually shows that one must sacrifice the inner self for worldly success or preserve the inner being at the cost of worldly ruin. Chapin has indeed sacrificed his inner being; he has alienated his children and a wife who loved him passionately, lost any sense of who he truly was, and not even grabbed the gold ring in the process.

Like Salinger's ending and Warden's plan to keep Prewitt from being charged with murder, Joe's affair does not promise a brighter world, but it questions whether life has to be as bad as Joe Chapin made it. The negatives of the book—the perversity of political machinery, the decline of aristocratic privilege, the relentless motion of time that leaves behind those who don't heed it—are diminished by the positive potential of romance.

Though Joe's compensation comes in a clumsily unmotivated affair, it suggests that obstructions to happiness are not entirely in the external world. The political machinery, though corrupt, has not ruined Joe's life, nor has he done it himself by ignoring platforms, programs, or people, nor by misreading opportunities which would have expedited his entry into public life.[30]

Possibilities for recuperation in a middlebrow novel are borrowed from highbrow or lowbrow structure. Prewitt takes the law into his own hands, and, had he retained that "larger than life" highbrow personality, he might have gotten away with murder; Chapin "gets the girl"—a lowbrow phenomenon—but he's too self-absorbed to keep her. By Prewitt's self-abandonment and Chapin's self-indulgence readers are given less demoralizing accounts of human possibility than what McCarthy offers in *The Group*. McCarthy may have been attempting to be more realistic; without providing some kind of recuperative possibilities, she is, in fact, being less literary. Still, strict middlebrow resolution, like Howe's *Circle of the Day* (exercise self-control: grin and bear it), results in pretty dull books.

That is not to say that better middlebrow novels result from breaking more middlebrow rules, as Ayn Rand's *Atlas Shrugged* clearly shows. Rand's agenda is socially relevant middlebrow. She aims to demonstrate how government interference prevents talented and committed people from achieving the kind of success they're capable of. One could even say that in her conception of Dagny Taggert, Hank Rearden, and other members of the Galt clan, Rand follows Lukács's formula for modern novel heroes: "In a world abandoned by God, the problematic individual . . . proceeds courageously to fight evil forces that make reality narrower than he wants it" (97).

To accomplish that aim, Rand first reverses the usual middlebrow pattern by making her protagonists actively struggle *against* the powers that be rather than attempting to break into their ranks. Clearly designating "enemies" gives the plot a lowbrow twist, which she reinforces by making the "good guys" handsome, brilliant, and strong, rather than typical. The "bad guys" are weak, snivelling, unintelligent, and unattractive: Wesley Mouch, the head of the government's "anti-dog-eat-dog" plan, is a man whose family "had known neither poverty nor wealth nor distinction for many generations."[31]

Government decisions are always ill-considered, petty, and anti-productive. American leaders resort to torture as a means of controlling dissidents. Like a silly parody of *1984*, *Atlas Shrugged* mimics philosophical legitimacy with the sixty-page speech on fascist doctrine, for example.[32] The fantastical hidden valley refuge of "Galt's Gulch," is no middlebrow lost Eden, but an entirely new Eden where people can be aggressive and self-serving and still find the oneness of community (and where, incidentally, lovely Dagny Tabbert will be the only unattached female among a horde of handsome unattached men).

Rand's implication that the dream world is viable rather than evanescent distorts the usual middlebrow option of success *in* the world or peace *outside* of it. Some might want to argue that Rand is a more vital social critic than McCarthy, Salinger, or Jones for suggesting that the world is too thwartive to bear and the only possibility for human survival in contemporary America is escape. The problem is that the retreat into Galt's Gulch is not fantastical *enough*. It is meant to provide the Galt gang the opportunity to consolidate their forces and come back to rebuild an America destined to fall in their absence. Promising a reclamation reduces the novel's capacity to critique contemporary culture.

Successful fifties middlebrow writers knew that social critique didn't work unless the depiction was realistic. What Rand may be doing instead is foreshadowing the development of a blended lowbrow/middlebrow genre that we see currently in the novels of Michael Crichton and John Grisham, who write of worlds of work gone so far awry that scrupulous people cannot participate in them without self-annihilation. Still, Grisham's readers know that Mitchell and Abby McDeere are *not* going to wait it out in the Caymans so that they can set America back on track.

The fragility or lostness of the dreamworld in novels like *Ten North Frederick, The Man in the Gray Flannel Suit*, and *From Here to Eternity* also foreshadow an era wherein walking the fine line of accommodation is just too difficult. The consolation prizes of Tom Rath and Joe Chapin were perhaps more easily swallowed by a fifties readership for whom economic growth was a real possibility, less easily by a nineties audience that fears for its own earning potential. Fifties readers were not deluded that the lucky breaks of Joe Chapin and Tom Rath depicted the way the world worked, but they were probably more willing to accept the uncomfortable implication that accommodation is required—because in the fifties accommodation paid off. In the nineties, to use Rand's phrase, it's a "dog-eat-dog" world.

NOTES

1. Several works in psychology and religion have this title, the most well known being R. D. Laing's, *The Divided Self* (New York: Pantheon, 1960), a discussion of schizophrenia. The title comes from a lecture in William James's, *Varieties of Religious Experience: A Study in Human Nature* (1902; New Hyde Park, NY: University Books, 1963), 168-188. James explains that humans suffer from an inability to match inner impulses to outwardly acceptable behavior so that "Peace cannot be reached by simple addition of pluses and minuses from life," but only through a "conversion experience," which is something like the concept of recuperation used in this chapter.

2. Morris Dickstein, "Popular Fiction and Critical Values: The Novel as a Challenge to Literary History," in Bercovitch, 37.

3. *Pleasure of the Text*, trans. Richard Miller (New York: Hill and Wang, 1975), 47.

4. "Write, She Said," in Radford, 227. Tania Modleski takes this one more turn in her complaint that the Oedipal underpinnings of all "classic narrative" disable the female [by casting her in the role of the nurturer?] and assert male superiority. *Loving with a Vengeance: Mass-Produced Fantasies for Women* (Hamden, CT: Archon, 1982), 15.

5. *Pleasure of the Text*, 6 and 29-35; *Image, Music, Text*, trans. Stephen Heath (New York: Hill and Wang, 1977), 9, 64. Brian Wicker suggests a similar capacity of language, when it is seen as an "agent, not an inert treasury." *The Story-Shaped World: Fiction and Metaphysics: Some Variations on a Theme* (Notre Dame, IN: U of Notre Dame P, 1975), 19.

6. This concept is fundamental to Lévi-Strauss's work, but spelled out specifically in the introduction to *The Raw and the Cooked*, trans. J. Weightman and D. Weightman (1964; New York: Basic, 1969).

Another myth-related solution is suggested by Frank Kermode: "Since all ways are barred," the novel requires that we fulfill the desires of the lower mind (provide closure in time) and adhere to the facts of reality. *Sense of an Ending* (1969; New York: Oxford UP, 1977), 135, 64.

7. *Theory of the Novel*, trans. Anna Bostock (Cambridge, MA: MIT P, 1971), 97.

8. Lukács says that "The form of the novel requires that the hero finds out through experience that a mere glimpse of meaning is the highest life has to offer and the only thing by which the struggle will be justified" (80). LeMaire says that "Every object of desire is necessarily ephemeral because it is incapable of stopping the lack" (175).

"Nowhere has man discovered a means of connecting himself to society except in the form of a truce with it. The best we have been able to do is to speak of a 'duty' to society, and this implies sacrifice or self-deprivation." Arthur Miller, Introduction to *A View from the Bridge* entitled "On Social Plays" (New York: Viking, 1955), 6.

9. Barthes would probably call this a novel of *plaisir* rather than *jouissance* because it "links comfortably with the ego and the culture." *Image, Music, Text* (14). D.G. Hoffman might call it the "transformation without rebirth" typical of "achieving identity in an egalitarian society." *Form and Fable in American Fiction* (Chicago: Henry Regnery, 1951), 79-80.

10. "Keats' American Dream," *America* (12 March 1960), 708. Sisk also wonders whether obsession with sex in American fiction is a (confused) instinctive attempt to protect freedom.

11. *Mythologies*, trans. Annette Lavers (New York: Hill and Wang, 1972), 14.

12. "Only an Occasional Rutabaga," *Modern Fiction Studies* 15 (Winter 1969-70): 471.

13. J.M. Rice credited Howe with "keen insight into a woman's life"; *Commonweal* (16 June 1950), 254. F. H. Bullock praised her "keen observation and skilled craftsmanship." The *New York Herald Tribune*, 21 May 1950, Book Rev: 4. But Leo Lerman of the *New York Times* says that she "never goes deep enough"; 28 May 1950, 18; and Elizabeth Janeway in the *Saturday Review of Literature*, says that the book is "sterile" because Howe "controlled her work too completely"; 20 June 1950, 33.

14. However, real powerlessness probably explains the superiority of *Main Street* to *Babbitt*, for Carol Kennicott seems more genuinely trapped and panicked by her situation than George Babbitt, for whom real and apparent escape hatches abound.

15. William Styron, *The Long March* (New York: Random, 1952), 119-20.

16. Lukács, 30.

17. Donald Barr says that *Catcher in the Rye* is a story about "an apprentice saint and his indignant love for this bad world" (28) and that Holden "excites our pity, makes us ashamed and enchants us." "Ah, Buddy: Salinger," in Balakian, 55.

18. *The Landscape of Nightmare: Studies in the Contemporary American Novel* (New York: NY UP, 1965), 56.

19. Bruce Bawer, who finds Salinger "congenitally less interested in getting to the bottom of his characters' emotionally retarded behavior than in celebrating it," concedes that the "vanity, solipsism, egocentrism, and unconscious hypocrisy are more easily forgivable, less psychopathic in Holden than they'd be in an older person." *Diminishing Fictions: Essays on the Modern American Novel and Its Critics* (St. Paul: Graywolf, 1988), 172 and 182.

20. Richard Ohmann observes that in this book childhood is the only defense against capitalist and socialist patriarchal social relations, where "visions of wholeness linger in memory and animate desires, but they collide with the main experiences of adult life." "The Shaping of the Canon: U.S. Fiction: 1960-1975," *Criticism* 10.1 (1983): 214-16.

21. Journalism is what Tom Wolfe is arguing for in "Stalking the Billion-Footed Beast," *Harper's* (November 1989). Part of Wolfe's rationale is that "truth is stranger than fiction"—that readers will get more information and insight from "legitimate" case studies than from artfully fictionalized ones (56).

Nelson Goodman argues that representation is always a form of classifying rather than imitating, so we're always doing some kind of characterizing rather than merely telling. *Language of Art: Approach to a Theory of Symbols* (Indianapolis: Hackett, 1976), 231.

Nevertheless, reportage has camp followers besides Tom Wolfe. One will commonly find the same book, *From Here to Eternity*, for example, praised for its thoroughness and condemned for its "welter of details" (see chapter five).

22. In *American Social Fiction*, Michael Millgate praises Salinger as one of the "few American writers who have seen man and society in proper proportion." (Edinburgh: Oliver, 1964), 204.

23. In a review of *Typical American* by Gish Jen, Daniel Max points out that while successful women authors of the seventies and early eighties "established a new kind of egotistical and unfeeling male," this portrait "eventually descended into cliché and from there into disuse. . . . [T]he voices that now find most admirers . . . have burned off the old anger—look at Anne Tyler's *Breathing Lessons*, for instance"; *Minneapolis Star Tribune* (28 April 1991), 9f. I cite this review as an example of how we describe our frustration in faddish ways.

24. (New York: Dell, 1963), 11.

25. Mary McCarthy, *The Group* (1954; New York: Signet, 1963), 218. All further quotations will be cited from this edition.

26. Benjamin DeMott, "Polls, Presidents and Preceptors." *Harper's* (October 1963), 98. Norman Podhoretz says that "Good people don't fit in her world: all activities are equally absurd, all people equally ridiculous." "Gibbsville and New Leeds: The America of John O'Hara and Mary McCarthy," *Commentary* (21 March 1956), 271.

However, Granville Hicks claims that *The Group* has "a quality that one has not come to expect from this particular author . . . compassion." *Saturday Review* (31 August 1963), 19.

27. "The modern, ambitious, opinionated girls lose," and "their ideas and possessions are made to seem pitiful," George Soule laments; McCarthy's "wit has lost its humanity" in this novel. "Must a Novelist Be an Artist," *Carleton Miscellany* (Spring 1964), 93-95.

28. Podhoretz says O'Hara is a "dutiful realist" who "creates a plausible likeness of the world" with characters "exhaustively defined by observable behavior" (269-70). Frederich Karl complains that "even at his best" O'Hara "skimmed surfaces—accumulating external details to avoid analysis." *American Fictions: 1940-1980: A Comprehensive Historical and Critical Evaluation* (New York: Harper, 1983), 125.

29. John O'Hara, *Ten North Frederick* (New York: Bantam, 1955), 355. Further quotations will be cited from this edition.

30. R.G. Davis argues that O'Hara's book works in spite of flaws: "There are two kinds of impelling truth in O'Hara's fiction . . . about the nature of much social behavior and about the nature of our concern with other people's lives. Both are partial truths and expressed with deliberate imaginative limitations which have kept O'Hara's work from developing, but [which are] disturbing and dangerous to deny." *New York Times Book Review* (27 November 1955), 1.

31. Ayn Rand, *Atlas Shrugged* (New York: Signet, 1957), 503-04. These phrases indicate the negative effects of dogmatism on writing style. All further quotations will be cited from this edition.

32. Waldmeir accuses Rand of "deadly serious Rightness" (473).

VII

HIGHBROW, LOWBROW, AND THE LAW

The previous chapter explains that one feature common to lowbrow, middlebrow, and highbrow novels is their struggle to reunite a self split between what is desired by intuition and what is learned or sanctioned by the social order.[1] Entry into the social order cannot occur without repression of felt desires. Lukács suggests that only the epic, wherein "Life and essence are identical," has the capacity to unify these divided aspects of human identity: where the epic thrives, human beings cannot desire "what the gods do not ordain."[2]

Although Lukács does not make this distinction, it seems that what comes between the era of the epic and the era of the novel is what the Western world might call the era of the Law—as prescribed in the teaching of the Torah or the Old Testament. The epic gods of and in nature become the God of the Word and construct a reunion between the spirit and the social self by training the spirit that the means of reunification with the Great Spirit is *conformity* to the *law*. Self-control becomes the heroic capacity. Scheman's Cartesian analysis suggests something like this:

> The Cartesian God . . . conscripts the infinite will of the privileged son and sets it the task of 'autonomously' disciplining the body, the perceptions and the passions, with the promised reward being the revelation of guaranteed truths and the power that goes with knowledge.[3]

In less academic or more religious circles, the reward is membership in the community of the elect or reunion with the "father in heaven."

In middlebrow structure characters do what they have to do to maintain a viable place in the economic order; they face reality and sideline the needs of the self—file them away as lost Edens—in order to cut their losses in the economic realm. Or else they reject as insufficient the compensations of the external world and fulfill the needs of the inner self come what may. Lowbrow characters do what they must to succeed in the *social* order; their private anxieties are displaced by submitting to the standard practice of the law, and they attain membership in the company of the "elect."

Highbrow characters resist both alternatives: they seek fruition that does not require compromise or submission to the law, yet they (and/or readers) come to learn the unattainability of such a goal. Their relationship to the law is ambivalent, for they know that its promise is deceptive and self-effacing, but that lawlessness is not the answer either. Often, an attempt to return to the law fails because there is no clear indication of what the law requires or who the "father" is. I use "father" to invoke our common sense of moral order; in a patriarchy it's hard to avoid the term, especially when dealing with fifties novels, in which the overt theme of "search for a father" is surprisingly prevalent—as the ensuing discussion will show. In any case, the law affects both lowbrow and highbrow recovery.

Lowbrow love for the law stems from its promise that the social realm is orderly, that it rewards selflessness and punishes selfishness, and that it's *worth it* to deny the self. Lowbrow stories are told in terms of rewards that a vast audience will recognize as rewards. Sexual satisfaction and socially acceptable marriage are fifties rewards for both sexes, as well as being respected rather than famous, honorable rather than rich. Having a good job or doing a good job were also male rewards, but not female.

Conformity to standard ethics looks less prohibitive in men's novels, for putting your life on the line, putting others' safety and success before your own, and not using people are culturally honorable acts, besides being adventurous and stimulating. In women's novels, not being aggressive, not insisting on your own way, not enticing or coveting, and giving up everything for the right man take the form of stultifying clichés. By cultural and commercial coding these rewards lose their essence as factors which connect to decency, self-restraint, and the standard wisdom of unselfish maturity. They become more clearly "worth it" through contrast to heroine's doubles, who are frequently undone by exhibiting the opposite traits of aggression, self-interest, and wanton unconcern for others' happiness and well-being.[4]

Lowbrow novels are often attacked because they seem to pose

solutions to the anxiety of the divided self and dissuade readers from doing anything to change dominant conditions. This Marxist and sometimes feminist critique treats literature as potentially *instrumental* in curing social ills and disparages unrealistic literature for undermining this potentiality. I see literature as potentially instrumental on a personal and individual level: If literature promotes a sense of recuperation, it is of the divided *self* not of a divided citizenship. I don't think *fiction* moves our social selves to work for the reparation of civil breaches, and I don't think readers of fiction make very good politicians.

Critics who focus on lowbrow rewards are bound to choke, for example, on the notion that Allison and Constance MacKenzie will both forget all the evils of the world and live happily ever after with their new lovers. But, as the *Peyton Place* analysis of chapter one shows, lowbrow recuperation is complicated by plot structure: the happy ending does not obliterate a world that promises little, and it disperses the bleaker, more realistic fates among doubled characters. Like the lost Edens of a middlebrow novel, the secondary elements of lowbrow novels challenge the false recovery that the protagonist's reward suggests. It's obviously easier to recognize highbrow ambiguity, irony, structure, and ambivalence because it's left on display, available for discussion. Self-annihilation is a price for embracing the law in both lowbrow and highbrow novels, but the focus is different: lowbrow foregrounds apotheosis and obscures annihilation, while highbrow does the opposite.

The lowbrow hero resists the law by accident, through fear or ignorance: she returns to the program of the law after having transgressed it mistakenly or overlooked it in favor of immediate security or irresistible temptation. One might call this unconscious resistance, and the highbrow hero's conscious, for the highbrow hero pointedly rejects the law as being too confining, too narrow to satisfy the needs of a self that's too big for such confinement. Or else the hero feels obliged to obey a law but doesn't know what it is.

In Leon Uris's lowbrow novel *Exodus*, the heroine is ignorant of the story's law that the ultimate good lies in serving a free and independent state of Israel, where Jews can live safe, productive, and tradition-sanctioned lives. The recovery pattern of this novel requires that she realize that achieving that good depends on everyone's willingness to sacrifice for the common cause. Even though innocent people must die in the effort, every bit of land reclaimed from Arab possession is a bit of the Garden of Eden.

Mrs. Kitty Fremont, pediatric nurse, gentile, widow, and mother whose only child is dead, resists cooperating because she thinks it's none of her concern. Although she delays returning to her job in the United States in order to assist three hundred refugee orphans, she agrees only because she wishes to adopt Karen, an orphan who resembles her daughter, before she returns. She resists pressures from Ari Ben Canaan, a military leader of the free state of Israel movement, to commit herself to Israel and to him. Instead she cherishes thoughts of returning to a lifestyle which had served her well in the past, and, until they are tested, she believes her standards are the right ones.

For Kitty Fremont, Ari Ben Canaan becomes a prophet of a new order more than a lover (though he must be a lover in a 1950s lowbrow novel; to make him merely a prophet or teacher would diminish his function as cultural symbol and foreclose on Kitty's potential reward). She responds immediately to his sexual attractiveness; yet she fears his hardness and determination, when, for example, he issues a proclamation that ten orphans will die each day until the *Exodus* is allowed to leave Cyprus and head for Israel. Her real reluctance to join spirits with Ari is her awareness that he "could defeat her,"[5] for she doesn't want to live her life "as a noble mission" other than being "needed by the man she loves" (444).

Two things finally motivate her decision to remain in Israel. First, Ari Ben Canaan gets critically wounded in guerrilla warfare, and the only skilled medic available is Kitty. She at last has the chance to be needed by this man whose habit is to give rather than receive. Second, after the British have withdrawn without providing the protection they'd promised, Arab attacks on Israeli entrenchments escalate to such a pitch that nothing short of heroic commitment from every man, woman, and child can stop their repossession of the newly chartered state.

As she is packing to leave for America, she rereads from a letter she had written to a friend: "The reason we are able to get such quick recoveries . . . [is the] wonder drug. . . 'Eretz Israel.'. . . They desire only to live and fight for their country," and she decides that she belongs in Israel (450-51). She wavers when Karen is killed, but Dov, Karen's fiancé, counsels her that " 'God wants His people . . . to guard His laws. . . . Israel is the bridge between darkness and light.'" Uris reports that "Suddenly Kitty saw . . . the answer. Israel, the bridge between darkness and light" (589).[6]

When Ari professes love for Kitty, he warns her that "It may be years . . . before I can . . . say that my need for you comes first, before all other things. . . . Will you be able to understand that?" Kitty will understand. At the Seder following this proposal, Dov reads: "On this night we celebrate their going forth in triumph from slavery into freedom" (599). Though Kitty has renounced her own creed, she has gained a sense of who she is that does not require her to have a child, be tidy and well-dressed, or possess a man.

It's too bad for those who would defend this denouement that she has to see the light via connection to a man,[7] when what wins her is connection to a *creed* or a law that tells her to put broader motives above her own and to sense her own and other individuals' insignificance in the good life. Rather than being defeated, she's transfigured by becoming part of "a noble mission."

Something similar happens, though more mundanely, in Lane Kauffmann's novel, *Six Weeks in March*. Connie Marshall, like Kitty Fremont, refuses to abandon her own prerogatives for someone else's: she has taken up a six weeks' residence in Reno to arrange a divorce from a husband she considers weak and carping and jealous of her superior abilities as an editor in their jointly run publishing company. Furthermore, she's got a new lover—a famous novelist. Her husband acquires a similar disposition by reviving an affair with a woman sexier and more yielding than Connie. Reviewing Connie's immature behavior, Don Marshall convinces himself that they're well parted.

Kauffmann's denouement is even harder to defend than Uris's, for it turns on a series of sexist bromides. To Connie's discomfiture, her Reno landlady, Mrs. Cutler, assumes that Connie deserves blame for the impending divorce, for "by her birthright" a woman has "a sensitivity to emotional states, a creative sympathy, a flair for composing atmospheres and refining relationships . . . if she chooses to exercise them."[8]

The clichés Cutler spouts function like the creed which motivates Jews in *Exodus* to give up everything for the State. And the spirit seems equally infectious, for Don capitulates as well:

> "Connie's hideously thoughtless and I'm hypercritical; . . . I win most of the arguments . . . and that helps convince me I'm in the right. . . . I feel that Connie is nine-tenths responsible for our troubles, but I'm sure she feels the same about me." (169)

In the end, influenced by diplomatic letters from their seventeen-year-old son urging them to preserve the family, they accept mutual responsibility for their marital morass. Each aware of how they must change their own attitudes and behavior, they move from "darkness into light," and another "state" is preserved that requires at least semi-self-less commitment of all parties involved.

From a nineties perspective the blatant sexism undoubtedly looks uglier than it looked to a fifties audience, for whom the adages would conform to received wisdom. In any case, the happy ending is tempered by the realization that a couple cannot be their old smug selves and have a happy marriage.

For lowbrow protagonists the law intervenes or reveals itself as a means to recovery. And, because the law *names* the problem, the solution, and the desired reward, what appears to be recovered is reduced to cliché and symbol. That does not necessarily make the recovery less psychologically satisfying to readers. Though Umberto Eco says that "overcoded" lowbrow texts do not invite reader participation because the author has supplied all needed information,[9] the "transparency" of lowbrow language allows the subconscious to act upon the reading experience.

Regardless of the apparent "closedness" of the plot, readers still have the power to draw from their imaginations the interpretants which the author has given another name. Lowbrow writers create plot structures congruent with readers' internal structures to provide access to internal sites of recovery; what appears on the page is a map rather than a blueprint. Readers transform lowbrow texts into constructs that serve particular needs, though those constructs remain inaccessible to our powers of analysis and discussion. There is some openness.

The very similarity of lowbrow stories gives evidence for this. The 1988 novel *Alias Madam Doubtfire*, by Anne Fine, is virtually the same story as *Six Weeks in March*: a marriage is collapsing because each spouse fails to accept the other's value prima facie. Each wants to be allowed to behave according to their own reading of the law; each must learn that the well-being of the group (especially when it comprises kids) must precede their own self-interests.

The materials in each correspond to the more familiar conditions of each decade: in *Alias Madam Doubtfire* conflicts arise because a mother is too busy to do all of the things that contemporary "super-moms" must do; dad is underemployed because he can't put up with the kind of demands that his wife can. They suffer from too much stress and too little "personal space," just like most upwardly mobile families of recent decades. The Marshalls suffer more fifties kinds of interference: a general anxiety about women in positions of influence in the workplace, a vague angst about fulfillment through marriage.

Charlotte Bronn, heroine of Eileen Bassing's lowbrow novel, *Home Before Dark*, wants her marriage to Arnold Bronn to fulfill all her personal needs. Though he has shattered her self-esteem through a poorly disguised attraction to her stepsister Joan, Charlotte remains determined. She attempts to become Joan; she won Arnold in the first place by cultivating Joan's charms.[10] Reviving the same strategy, she dyes her hair and dresses for a dinner party in a gold lamé dress of the sort Joan would wear. Arnold's repulsion at this ludicrous mime brings her efforts at self-effacement to an end.

Bassing's novel is a fifties version of the Cyrano story, given a fifties spin by making Arnold a college professor, Charlotte a victim of shock treatments, domestication, and male domination. The story reappears in every generation (*When Harry Met Sally* is a recent film version). In each case the reader is provided with a scenario that is imminently replaceable. You can change the configuration with different clothing styles, a different number and age of children, a more timely set of male-female issues, but you get characters struggling with the issue of how to adapt their personal shortcomings in ways that will maintain membership in "the clan"—even the very small clan of marriage.

Where lowbrow protagonists look for a way *in*, highbrow protagonists look for a means to evade the self-annihilating requirements of the law and still have a place in the order of things. It's a given in highbrow structure that the protagonist will transgress the law, and a given that transgression will bring pain of some kind. The highbrow reader does not gain satisfaction through the appropriateness of the protagonist's fate, but in their own ability to comprehend that fate. Successful highbrow novels require active participation in figuring out why the protagonist ends up as s/he does. Highbrow and lowbrow acknowledge the same dominant law, but lowbrow accepts it as supportive, where highbrow does not trust its promise.

Typical highbrow heroes begin by seeing the world as wrong for *them*; recovery comes when they realize that they're not bigger than the social order. At the opening of *Henderson the Rain King*, Henderson details his sense of being larger than life: "Six feet four inches tall. Two hundred and thirty pounds. An enormous head. . . I am rich."[11]

For all his size, success, sex appeal, and fertility ("Christ, I've got plenty of children" [8]), he cannot quell the disturbance in his heart that says, "I want, I want, I want!" (24). Unlike Holden Caulfield, who sees the world as being too confining for anybody, Henderson sees only his own plight. What satisfies an ordinary man does not satisfy Henderson. And so he goes to Africa, a place he sees as "discontinuous with civilization" (279), to attempt to silence this voice.[12] At the end of that trip, the voice stills as he recognizes an order in which he is but a cipher, a coextensive element. He achieves peace with the universe by learning his own littleness in it.

Henderson's ego precipitates his education. In a rain-making ceremony wherein the "rain-maker elect" cannot lift the heavy wooden statue called Mummah, Henderson feels he must try, though he has no idea of the significance of the feat. He knows merely that he wants to test his strength. He succeeds, and when rain falls shortly thereafter, he is designated "Rain King," heir to the present king's throne.

Dhafu begins to teach Henderson what his job involves. Understanding the lion is most important, since Henderson's biggest test will be to capture the lion supposed to contain the preceding king's soul. When Henderson absorbs lion into himself, Dhafu says, he will learn to distinguish "the states that are given and the states that are made" (221-23).[13]

Dhafu tells him that he came to Africa because "You did not believe you had to perish" (219) and teaches him that he must go from "man-want-to-live" to understanding how to die.[14] To that end, Dhafu undergoes a "sacrificial death" in order that Henderson may develop completely; in this chapter's terms, he becomes the "father."[15] By this time Henderson has learned that he doesn't want the job. To be special is to court death. Henderson sees that stature not only does not bring an end to mortality, it expedites it. But it is no longer death he fears. When he chooses to resume his place *in time*, in the *continuous* part of civilization, we can suppose that he accepts his own mortality.

In the novel's final scene, Henderson is flying back to reunite with his wife in New York. He has brought a lion cub with him, a reminder of Dhafu's soul and of his own mortality. Henderson befriends an orphan, and, when the plane stops for refueling in Newfoundland, he bundles the little boy in a blanket and runs with him in exuberant circles around the plane:

> Laps and laps I galloped around the shining and riveted body of the plane. . . . Dark faces were looking from within. The great beautiful propellers were still, all four of them. I guess I felt it was my turn now to move, and so went running—leaping, leaping, pounding, and tingling over the pure white lining of the gray Arctic silence. (286)

The life-in-death equivocation is almost overstated here.[16] In this cold, colorless, sterile environment, father and "son" perform a circle dance to their endlessness and oneness. Yet the plane, with propellers poised to whirl them back into time, is full of "dark faces" that watch their charade, and the lion who bespeaks Henderson's fate sleeps in its belly. This is a frozen rather than fecund moment in time. The return to New York will start the propellers whirling and wake the sleeping beast; it will rekindle the sense of loss and distance.

The inevitable reentry into the *continuous* world accentuates the merely momentary power of the mind to distance itself from a world that's too much with us as we approach the reintegration of the sundered halves of the soul. Again, *art* becomes the solution as it did for Humbert in *Lolita*, for "art redivides time" and merges the moment with eternity.[17] As Lukács puts it, *composition* reveals that apparent organicism is illusory. A new perspective recognizes the independence of parts as well as their attachment to the whole. That whole is never organic, merely conceptual, abolished again and again.[18]

Bellow indulges lowbrow fantasy and overdeterminism in having Dhafu spell out the lessons Henderson must learn,[19] but recoups the highbrow program of elusive satisfaction through Dhafu's predictable death and the ironic ending.[20] Highbrow novels always recognize that one can be at peace neither within nor without the order of the law; one can at best understand that this is so and occasionally glimpse a world, like the frozen turf of Newfoundland, where unity is possible.

Like a lowbrow novel, however, the recovery in *Henderson* has little to do with social critique. There is not so much a "separate peace" from the slings and arrows of outrageous fortune (middlebrow), as there is a decidedly personal peace, just as in lowbrow. That it is not to say that highbrow novels never comment on social conditions, for, as I said in chapter four, one branch of American highbrow, in the tradition of Twain and James, sees the exterior world as the block to the soul's recuperation.

I mentioned earlier in this chapter that the search for a father seems to be a predominant theme of fifties novels. The inability to find a dependable role model seems to be a chief cultural indictment of the American fifties, exemplified by Nabokov's *Lolita*. The fifties is perhaps obsessed with the theme because this end of the blue-collar community and dawning of Whyte's corporate "social ethic" made us cognizant of the instability of our moral underpinnings. The fifties was also a more naive era than the present, when we still felt that we could redeem civilization if we knew whom to follow. Novelists were perhaps also foreshadowing the cultural situation we now find ourselves in, where the sense of "fathers" as spokespersons for the "master narratives" that hold social structure together seems irretrievable.

James Purdy's *Malcolm* features this indictment as well, for its protagonist seems completely victimized by a world devoid of law and fathers.[21] The climax of the novel occurs when Malcolm curtails the wait for a second "father" to show up. Girard Girard, who has expressed an interest in adopting Malcolm, has not materialized several hours after the appointed time, so Malcolm accepts a ride from a motorcyclist and from that point gives his life over to the whims of a hedonistic rock star. That he dies from overindulgence of the flesh seems the direct result of his inability to "find a father."

Helen, Milton, and Peyton Loftis in Styron's *Lie Down in Darkness* are another cast of characters suffering "moral bewilderment and unfocussed anxiety" that prevent them from acknowledging and dealing with the "contest between moribund moral imagination and sheer animal survival instinct."[22] Like children rather than responsible members of a family unit, each fixes obsessively on a substitute "reward" for leaving the "smothering orbit of infantile protection."[23] Helen cleaves to "the broken image of herself" in her retarded daughter Maudie; Milton uses Dolly Bonner as a vicarious stand-in for his incestuous interest in Peyton, and Peyton "sublimates her 'Electra complex'" by killing herself instead of Helen.[24] Milton and Peyton deny their desire for "the enchantment of infancy" through alcohol and substitute lovers, Helen through religion.[25] The novel ends at the scene of a black congregation's immersion baptism rite—a suggestion that it's necessary to abandon the self before you can arise.

John Hawkes's *The Cannibal* shows characters who *choose* blindness as a means of coping with their surrealistic, anarchic world of war-torn Germany. Their failure to pay attention to one another and their insistence on serving only their own needs mark a self-absorption that blights the human soul. Stella Snow's suffocation of her weakling husband and especially the Duke's slaughter of Jutta's son are telling examples of willful blindness. Germany provides the backdrop of a "fatherland" that has shirked its duty to lead its children out of darkness.

In the "search for a father," lowbrow protagonists know or learn what the law is and who to pattern themselves after. The "truth" often turns out not to be what the character wanted or expected, but once it's apparent, it's irrefutable (as is Kitty's revelation that Israel is "the answer"). Like the Marshalls, they may have to give up cherished notions about themselves in adapting to the law, but "rewards" make evident the rightness of doing so.

The law or father is elusive in highbrow fiction; recovery is imaginative or evanescent (as in *Henderson*) or it is evasive and intangible. No revelation is available to Frank Alpine in Bernard Malamud's *The Assistant*. Frank Alpine has both bad and good role models, but he has no wizard or magic to help him decide which is which.[26] So he becomes something of a Jekyll and Hyde, part Francis of Assisi[27] dedicated to brotherly coexistence, part embittered street thug with a compulsion to take what he thinks the world withholds from him.

His "bad angel" ("bad self" by Proppian doubling) is Ward Minogue, the son of a local police detective who banished Ward from his sight when he could not beat out of him the urges to steal and mug. His father's hardness attenuates Ward's culpability, for by refusing to talk to or see Ward, the elder Minogue deprives him of the law and a father and, symbolically therefore, of the chance to get it right.

Morris Bober, an aging, failed grocer, makes a similarly ambiguous "good angel," for though he is a man of humility, responsibility, and kindness,[28] he is "unwilling to adapt to an increasingly opportunistic culture."[29] His notion of what it means to be a Jew is "to suffer."[30] Frank's first encounter with Morris Bober comes in assisting Minogue's armed robbery of Bober's little grocery.

Bober becomes Alpine's good angel when he accepts Frank's offer to help out in the store for practically no pay. He entrusts Frank with trying out new ideas to improve the business and gives him fatherly advice. But, once he's worked his way into Bober's confidence, Frank steals milk from him and takes to sleeping in Bober's cellar without permission. "Disturbed by his own selflessness," because it "represents a loss of identity," he starts to steal money from the till as well.[31] Then he starts to put it back in. He maintains a friendship with Minogue, who continues to urge him to assist in other jobs.

His ambivalent relationship to the world is mirrored in his treatment of Bober's twenty-four-year old daughter Helen. From the very first, Frank views Helen as too good for him. Because he allows himself to hope for nothing more, he shimmies up an air shaft to her second-story bathroom, to gaze on her as she undresses:

> He felt . . . an overwhelming desire to love her, at the same time
> an awareness of loss, of never having had what he had wanted

most. . . . He felt greedy as he gazed. . . . But in looking he was forcing her out of reach, making her into a thing only of his seeing, her eyes reflecting his sins . . . his passion poisoned by his shame. . . .[32]

Helen symbolizes all that Frank wants and can't have, and when it appears that she actually is falling in love with him, as if to affirm his sense that the world cannot reward the likes of him, he scotches his chances by literally becoming Ward Minogue—raping her moments after saving her from Ward's assault. By itself, this scene illustrates the forces of the divided self. Frank's id wants a fleshly experience of Helen that the superego has told him he cannot have, so by forcing himself upon her he satisfies both—by having her and precluding the possibility of having her again.

At the end of *The Assistant*, Bober has died and Frank is manager of the grocery store. Though he has somewhat mended fences with Helen, he has not pursued the education he told Helen he craved, and he has not turned the business around as he thought he might. A hopeful sign is that Ward Minogue has died. And Frank has had himself circumcised—a richly ambiguous gesture. Ostensibly it shows that he wants to make himself an acceptable mate for Helen rather than the "uncircumcised dog" she called him after the rape. But the circumcision is also symbolic castration, a means to atone for the rape, to exorcise Ward Minogue, and to become the passive saint whose life and character always intrigued him.[33] In this new state, he seems more a reincarnated Bober than a future husband for Helen,[34] but the act shows that he "continues to desire the closure" of the gap between self and the world.[35]

Frank's "changing places" with Morris Bober partly fulfills that desire by showing the collapsibility of roles—a carnivalesque turn which makes the characters less individual, less "outside" each other, more a part of Bakhtin's "immortal crowd."[36] Such a melding seems very much like the submergence of self that occurs in lowbrow recuperation.

But the fact that Frank *approaches* the closure rather than *achieves* it is essential in fending off his annihilation. Lowbrow recuperations fend off absorption into the "immortal crowd" because the protagonists' doubled selves remain in less recovered worlds than the protagonists do. "The merely momentary power of the mind" to settle into any kind of surety accomplishes that aim in highbrow. Bellow's, Nabokov's, and Malamud's protagonists are made to vacillate between two worlds. Bellow's technique of using geographically separate worlds is more literal and thus trickier to integrate than Malamud's. Malamud's ways of splitting are more organic; the "divided self" of Frank's character, his exchangeability with Bober, Helen's hot and cold behavior toward men, the business that prospers and fails are structural markers.

And Malamud's writing is rich with textual markings of the same vacillation: "Malamud combines the colloquial and the mundane with the incantatory and religious . . . to fuse the assumptions of Marx with the patterns of myth." Nothing is ever settled, all is ambiguity, all is possibility; there is, says Schulz, "no clear victory" and less than a "full affirmation."[37] Neither despair nor optimism is called for, but only the willingness to continue to "desire the closure."

Unlike lowbrow protagonists, highbrow protagonists rarely find the key to undoing what is wrong about themselves, though they may recognize what is wrong about the world. *The Fixer* is Malamud's 1974 novel whose very title interrogates the possibility of fixing; the main character is, like Cheever's Falconer, a falsely accused protagonist who can do little to clear his name.[38] When Updike set his hero on the chase in 1961, Rabbit Angstrom couldn't find a place to come to rest until he was carried off to death in the wings of a pink armchair in 1991.

The search for fathers has been replaced in recent highbrow fiction metonymically, as in lowbrow replacement, with the search for a new world view, as witnessed by our interest in writers like Marquez, Allende, Borges, Morrison, and Erdrich. But a sense of disgruntlement about the order of the law has not mutated. There is a critique of the social order, but the fact that it is a *timeless* critique rather than a contemporaneous one makes highbrow fiction less valuable as a Marxist vehicle for social reform than some Marxists would wish.

Marxist critics have been less quick to condemn highbrow literature because highbrow novels overtly deny the value of membership in the dominant social orders. They think that lowbrow texts annihilate dissatisfaction because protagonists and readers are absorbed into dominant social strategies. I've tried to point out two reservations about that charge. One is that lowbrow characters are not so much conforming to negative social strategies as they are eliminating negative personal strategies. Heroes conquer personal obstacles rather than ignore social ones. The second is that the *world* of the lowbrow novel is made no better by the hero's reward than the world of the highbrow novel is made more corrupt by the hero's failure. An unmanageable world remains in place in both.

To argue similarity between highbrow and lowbrow fiction challenges Adorno and Horkheimer's complaint that the "culture industry" makes "individuals expendable and insignificant."[39] Their explicit rejection of lowbrow, besides overlooking a real human need to sometimes belong to "the immortal crowd," is challenged by sentiments, such as those of Jürgen Habermas's, that civilization might be saved by consensus communities wherein dialogue might foster a sense of togetherness that would suspend declining values. Frederic Jameson argues that, since capitalism has dissolved all the cohesiveness we need for group life, we need to look for it in "authentic art"—that which draws us by the virtue of *collectivity*.[40]

But real consensus is not possible, just as a real reunion of the divided self is not possible. What Habermas advocates is the kind of artificial and yet comfort-making waystation of lowbrow literature (and most television, according to Camille Paglia).[41] Jean-François Lyotard's *The Postmodern Condition* presents the more highbrow proposal that, living in an era which has lost faith in all "master narratives," we agree to live with instability.[42] What I've been suggesting in this chapter is that, contrary to academic opinion, both highbrow and lowbrow narratives allow us to do that.

NOTES

1. This is also the dichotomy Freud uses in *Civilization and Its Discontents*, trans. and ed. James Strachey (1930; New York: Norton, 1961).

2. Lukács, 30-34, 88, 119. In positing the unified world view of epic literature, Lukács seems guilty of middlebrow "Golden Age" nostalgia, but he does acknowledge that *form* achieves the desired dialectic: "The relation to redemption remains inexpressible because of . . . double servitude"—to norms rooted in an all-perfecting God and at the same time subject to historical/philosophical relativity (90-91).

It seems that our distance from the era of the epic expedites Lukács's view of the epic as truly integrated. Just as it's hard to imagine how the Egyptians built the Pyramids, it's hard to imagine how cultures forged epic certainty, but forged it must have been.

3. Naomi Scheman, *Engenderings: Constructions of Knowledge, Authority, and Privilege* (New York: Routledge, 1993), 95.

4. See chapter four.

5. Leon Uris, *Exodus* (New York: Bantam, 1958), 396. All further quotations will be cited from this edition.

6. Kent Bales has pointed out to me that during the fifties, as never before in American social history, the Jewish race became synonymous with qualities that their trials in Hitler's Europe revealed: patience, forbearance, humility, decency, selflessness.

7. In a *Midstream* review of this novel (Autumn 1961), Joel Carmichael says that there is "something deeply offensive about the popularity of this book." He's appalled by Uris's "bewildering lack of talent" and "abuse of English" and a plot which "reduces all collective ideas, symbols, and myths to . . . silliness" (86-9). Uris is no wordsmith and many turns of the plot (particularly the love affair between Fremont and Ben Canaan that ignites by spontaneous combustion and kindles without fuel during a phase of Ben Canaan's work when romance should be his last pursuit) look silly (by highbrow standards), but Uris doesn't lack talent. The ability to attract, absorb and affect millions of readers isn't Carmichael's notion of talent, but it is talent. Uris's books obviously give people something they want and/or need, something self-affirming and/or soul-soothing.

8. Lane Kauffmann, *Six Weeks in March* (New York: Avon, 1956), 179-80. All further quotations will be cited from this edition.

9. *The Role of the Reader: Explorations in the Semiotics of Texts* (1979; Bloomington: Indiana UP, 1984).

10. Eileen Bassing, *Home Before Dark* (New York: Random, 1957), 73-74.

11. Saul Bellow, *Henderson the Rain King* (New York: Avon, 1958), 8. All further quotations will be cited from this edition.

12. John Jacob Clayton notes that Henderson starts out full of destructive egoism because underneath he feels like one of the pigs he raises, having wrongfully survived his brother's drowning. He goes to Africa to escape "his sense of intrusion" and his mortality. *Saul Bellow: In Defense of Man* (Bloomington: Indiana UP, 1968), 171-72.

13. Marcus Klein says that Henderson "destroys himself body and soul to become a lion and learns about self-transformation, what it is to contain one's freedom." "A Discipline of Nobility," *Kenyon Review* (Spring 1962), 224.

14. Clayton calls Dahfu "Henderson's double," who shows him what it is to die with dignity" (178-82).

15. D.J. Hughes, "Reality and the Hero: *Lolita* and *Henderson the Rain King*," *Modern Fiction Studies* 6(Winter 1960-1): 359.

16. Roger B. Salomon calls this ending no real "resolution," but a "dialectic of the mock heroic." *Desperate Storytelling: Post-Romantic Elaboration of the Mock-Heroic Mode* (Athens: U of Georgia P, 1987), 233.

17. Max R. Schulz, *Radical Sophistication: Studies in Contemporary Jewish-American Novelists* (Athens, OH: Ohio UP, 1969), 117.

18. *Theory of the Novel*, trans. Anna Bostock (1920; Cambridge, MA: MIT P, 1971), 75-77.

19. K.K. Ruthven says that parts of this novel read like an orthodox quest novel; others like a parody of that. *Myth* (London: Methuen, 1976), 80. Hughes says parody "threatens to topple the whole enterprise" (346).

20. Clayton insists that it's an "affirmation too cheaply won" (185).

21. Anthony Burgess calls *Malcolm* an "allegory of growing up in an era which offers nothing." *The Novel Now* (London: Faber, 1967), 204.

Webster Schott says that Malcolm is desired and consumed by adults because he has innocence—what they've lost. "James Purdy: American Dreams," *Nation* (23 March 1964), 302.

Warren French calls Malcolm "the guiltless victim of a degenerate society." "The Quaking World of James Purdy," *Essays in Modern American Literature* (DeLond, FL: Stetson UP, 1960), 120.

22. David L. Stevenson, "Styron and the Fiction of the Fifties," *Critique* 3.3 (1960): 47.

23. Maxwell Geismar, *American Moderns from Rebellion to Conformity* (New York: Hill and Wang, 1958), 245.

24. Jonathan Baumbach, *Landscape of Nightmare: Studies in the Contemporary American Novel* (New York: New York UP, 1965), 125-30.

25. Geismar, 245.

26. Joseph Waldmeir calls Frank a medieval holy man in a wasteland who feels sin and guilt, but finds no system to guide him. "Only an Occasional Rutabaga," *Modern Fiction Studies* 15 (Winter 1969-70): 475-6.

27. This comparison is made both by Schulz and Robert Ducharme; *Art and Ideas in the Novels of Bernard Malamud* (The Hague: Mouton, 1974), 17.

28. Ducharme is one who sees Bober as "Christlike" (17). Robert Alter says that, as a father for Frank, Bober is the next best thing to Francis of Assisi, for Frank learns to be unselfish by attaching himself to Bober. *After the Tradition: Essays on Modern Jewish Writing* (New York: Dutton, 1969), 94.

29. Alter, 91.

30. Though Dickstein argues that "the schlemiel character in Jewish literature becomes a vehicle of transcendence," he believes that Malamud is a uniquely Jewish writer who sees, as Bober sees, being a Jew is to suffer, and the only proper response to that is quiet stoicism, stubborn decency—Bober's stock in trade. *Gates of Eden: American Culture in the Sixties* (New York: Penguin, 1977), 47-48.

31. Baumbach, 115.

32. Bernard Malamud, *The Assistant* (New York: Avon, 1957), 89-90. All further quotations will be cited from this edition.

33. Ducharme calls the circumcision a submission of the ego to the col-

lective superego, a sign that he accepts the moral value and authority of his "father" Morris (61).

34. A reading that is also justified by Frank's accidentally falling into Bober's grave and having to lift himself out (Baumbach 121).

35. Martin Green, "The Morality of *Lolita*," *Kenyon Review* 28 (1966), 375.

36. Mikhail Bakhtin, *Rabelais and His World*, trans. Helene Iswolsky (Cambridge, MA: MIT P, 1968), 256, 265.

37. Schulz, 57 and 62.

38. Some critics argue that the reconciliation is completed in Frank's circumcision and reincarnation as Bober, Baumbach says Frank achieves redemption, becoming "wholly honest and good" (121), renewing in his own spiritual rebirth "the saintly life of his exemplary father" (106). Ducharme feels that Frank, by learning from Bober to forsake "the selfish ambition for success in the world," has ascended into his true self as Francis of Assisi (17, 37). This reading gets a little support from its homophonic relation to the title.

39. Theodor W. Adorno and Max Horkheimer, "The Culture Industry: Enlightenment or Mass Deception," *Dialectic of the Enlightenment*, trans. John Cumming (New York: Continuum, 1986), 145.

40. Frederic Jameson, "Reification and Utopia in Mass Culture," *Social Text* 1 (1979), 140.

41. "Ninnies, Pedants, Tyrants, and Other Academics," *New York Times Book Review* (5 May 1991) sec. 7: 1+.

42. *The Post-Modern Condition: A Report on Knowledge*, trans. Geoff Bennington and Brian Massumi, Theory and History of Literature 10 (1979; Minneapolis: U of Minnesota P, 1984), xv-xvi.

VIII

MOPPING MY BROWS

I undertook this study because I wanted to know whether the fiction most of my students preferred to read was going to rot their brains and corrupt civilization. I had hoped that I would come to the end of this project prepared to argue that there was much to be gained from reading lowbrow and middlebrow fiction and to propose strategies that would assure worthwhile reading. I am prepared to do these things, but with a few more reservations than I had anticipated.

I've suggested, like Tony Bennett, that we need to pay more attention to the formal properties of popular fiction before we pass judgment on it.[1] Though Jauss argues that we automatically condition our reading practices according to whatever the text invites us to do,[2] Éva Federmayer suggests that we read in *programmed* ways, exercising prevailing naturalized reading strategies.[3] That prompts the first reservation.

If it is only the "learned reader" who decodes by classifying the works into genres,[4] then all that I've argued about variations in functions of highbrow, middlebrow, and lowbrow fiction won't be discovered unless readers are trained to read differing subgenres with differing mindsets. Readers who know the distinctions I've catalogued in this book won't, for example, automatically dismiss a novel because of its flat prose, for they would know that undistinguished prose works better in lowbrow novels than "good writing" does. Knowing that middlebrow novels generally require the recognition of a "lost Eden" helps us see that unrealistic plot turns sometimes work better than realistic ones. But it seems both unlikely and impractical that educators will undertake to teach subgenres in an era where we struggle just to get students to read. The kind of analysis I'm applying to middlebrow and lowbrow fiction is clearly the kind of analysis that "takes the fun out" of reading that students may yet see as fun.

My second reservation comes from our general inability or unwillingness to deny the correspondence between the word and the thing. Untrained readers tend to take for granted that what *looks* mimetic *is* mimetic, unless there are highbrow implicatures[5] signaling us to do otherwise. Therefore, we dismiss the awkward dialogue of middle-brow as just poor writing rather than a device to meld all characters into the typical, and we overlook the metonymic nature of lowbrow structure. Nabokov gives us signals, so we see incest in *Lolita* as artful metaphor; because Metalious doesn't, we read *Peyton Place* as smut.

We're willing to accept sex and violence in highbrow novels because we think they're somehow transformed by the operations that readers perform on them, and yet we deny the possibility that similar operations take place in lowbrow readings. Even Janice Radway, who worked to justify the reading tastes of romance readers, reiterates the difference: Literature's "internal operations are thought to deconstruct ideology whereas formulaic structures naturalize" the ideological by means of non-contradictory messages.[6]

To see something as metaphor requires a reader to deny the literal truth in order to perceive the real truth,[7] and this is difficult to do when we teach pupils to read all novels in relatively the same way and when lowbrow materials, by virtue of their generality, flaunt their connectedness to readers' lives. We may be more willing to work with highbrow language simply because highbrow writers *invite* us to, where lowbrow writers don't.

We're not *asked* to read Mike Hammer's words "Show em . . . we aren't so soft. . . . Kill, kill, kill, kill!" as anything but proof that Spillane's detective is blood-thirsty, subhuman, and unequivocally trigger-happy.[8] We see Hammer only as a "killer with delusions of grandeur," who revels in the power of a gun.[9]

In the opening scene of *One Lonely Night*, a judge ruefully dismisses charges against Mike Hammer, denouncing him as a man with "an ugly reputation . . . [and] no earthly reason for existing in a decent, normal society" (8). Hammer is typically viewed as he is by Christopher LaFarge, who calls Hammer's killings "sadism" and Spillane's fiction "immature and potentially destructive . . . wish-fulfillment."[10]

John C. Holmes, commenting on violence in "beat" novels, says these acts comprise "the sort of crime . . . which the cruel absence of God made obligatory if a man were to prove that he was a man and not a mere blot of matter." To Holmes, such violence expresses a longing for values, an attempt to achieve something meaningful.[11] Lukács says that, like madness, crime is a sign of homelessness.[12] Camille Paglia says violence in American culture expresses our primitivism and anarchic individualism.[13]

All of these analyses apply in some way to Mike Hammer's behavior, yet we respond more thoughtfully to Cross in Richard Wright's *The Outsider*, even though he kills with no remorse. Cross first becomes a killer to silence a man who may reveal that he's alive, when Cross wishes to be believed dead. Though his murders are less "justified" than Hammers', critics look for complex motivation here where they see only blood-lust in Hammer. Nathan A. Scott, Jr., says Cross is a man who sees "both Kurtz's 'horror' and the terrible joy of murderous orgasm."[14]

Our reaction may go beyond sympathy with "Ras, the Exterminator" from Ellison's well regarded highbrow novel, *Invisible Man*. Robert Bone says the novel's surrealistic, distorted, burlesque qualities penetrate "the two great illusions of the time—Stalinism and capitalism."[15] Anthony Burgess calls the novel Kafkaesque, symbolic, and allegorical, with apocalyptic visions.[16] Richard Kostelanetz sees its surrealism as promoting a kind of descent ritual.[17] Ras becomes something of a Manichaean prophet who opposes the Brotherhood's intellectualizing and encourages Harlem's denizens to murder, plunder, and burn. As Invisible Man becomes disillusioned with the Brotherhood's inconsistency, Ras's philosophies express an increasingly appealing alternative. When the Brotherhood makes IM "no longer a brother," the novel shows the possibility of conquering the agony of life through a toughness of spirit.[18] Hammer we see only as conquering an agony of spirit with a toughness of life.

It's easy to read Ellison's "Brotherhood" as a multi-purpose symbol—of white supremacists, of bankrupt Communist morality, and of suppressive membership in a flock. But it's hard to see beyond the redneck stereotyping of Spillane's "Commies" as competitive, deceitful thugs out to rule the world. Hammer's bragging doesn't dispel this impression: "I pumped slugs into the nastiest bunch of bastards you ever saw. . . . They were Commies, . . . red sons-of-bitches" (171). This quote illustrates the problem of *naming* and gives fodder to critics who see Hammer glorifying a McCarthyist desire that one man—himself— be the "privileged savior." Predictably, LaFarge sees Spillane's program as a cop-out: a "witch-hunt" to "obliterate rather than correct what we disapprove of" (12).

It takes some intellectualizing to see that a nameless frustration is given a name in "commies." John Searle says that names enable us to refer publicly without having to agree on what constitutes identity. He might call the invocation of "communism" here an "institutional fact" whose truth is determined by its position in a system.[19] Michael Millgate says that communism is one of the forms that have "institutionalized our sense of alienation in America."[20] Collins and Traylor defend the Hammer character as a "state of mind" which works on intuition rather than logic and brings to light attitudes and feelings one might try to hide.[21] They argue that Hammer's censorious judge represents a society that sends a man to war to defend that society and then hypocritically condemns him when he feels alienated by his inability to fight injustice when he's back home.[22]

Collins and Traylor see Hammer as a doubled character, not just a revenger, but also a hero in the Western mode, who kills to defend "God's justice."[23] Such a reading heightens the metaphorical potential of the communist issue in *One Lonely Night*, for it answers Hammer's question of whether he's cold-blooded: No, he just feels good about killing when he feels that his victims really deserve to die.

Still, even if we concede that this *name* speaks to individual readers of their own frustrations that are somehow brought to mind by the invocation of communism, we're left with having a term emblazoned on a reader's conscious mind as a *symbol* of all that's uncontrollable (just as we worry that the romance's perpetual symbol of *marriage* fuels readers' unrealistic dreams).[24]

What we need to do is explain the referent historically and not merely semantically. The symbols wouldn't work unless they were already part of mass consciousness; perception is always already representation.[25] The Rosenbergs were arrested in 1950; *One Lonely Night* was published in 1951. Communism symbolized our fears of a vulnerable social order throughout the fifties;[26] in the seventies it was replaced by a disdain for capitalists[27]—the opposite side of the same coin.

Symbols choose us rather than vice versa; they grab a mass consciousness because they're viable and handy at a particular moment. Marriage is always handy because it's been a cultural institution for so long. Especially since the Industrial Revolution diminished the extended family wherein all manner of kin might cohabit, marriage has also come to symbolize membership in a clan or tribe: it guarantees inclusion in a world with increasingly smaller tribes. In a theoretically class-

less capitalist society, marriage also, paradoxically, signifies self-determination, for choosing a marriage partner amounts to selecting a situation in the social realm. In the era of birth control and elective abortion,
having a baby becomes a marker of responsibility and indispensability
in a world that denies us the opportunity to make real contributions;
hence, besides the mushrooming of teenage mothers, we are seeing a
spate of popular movies featuring babies (for example, *Look Who's
Talking, Three Men and a Baby*). Vampires give substance to our sense
that we're being sucked of life by powers beyond our control; hence,
Anne Rice.

As I said in chapter five, lowbrow writers use *bricolage*, borrowing
whatever cultural pieces are at hand to give substance to that which is felt
rather than seen, to provide access to the concerns of the unconscious.
They engage readers' imaginations through these culturally loaded codes
as well as through coded turns of plot whose structures match patterns of
the subconscious and whose characters function typically. Thus, whereas
language itself signals the imaginative quality of highbrow texts, *structure*
signals the imaginative nature of lowbrow texts.

The images created by well chosen plot turns and functional characters serve in dream-like or rebus-like ways[28] and are always figurative
rather than literal. I'm talking here, of course, about something that we
can't fathom: "submerged text." Having steadily maintained that lowbrow novels engage the reader on a subconscious level by means of
image-access, I obviously assume that at least some of readers' textual
recovery takes place at a level inaccessible to analysis.

Theories about the subtextual level are interesting: Madonna
Miner posits that the subtext of women's novels is a bisexual triangle,[29]
which could either suggest that these novels appeal to aspects of
repressed sexuality or that they symbolize the Freudian process of re-
forming alliances in the maturation process. Another understanding of
subtext might be evolved from Helen Taylor's comment that *Gone with
the Wind* is a novel which "thrives on sexual ambivalence" with a heroine who is like a man in her refusal to have sex and bear children.[30]
Scarlett is, of course, another negative heroine whose "better half" of
Melanie Wilkes fulfills mature female obligations while Scarlett manages to cast off husbands and children like last year's dolls. The sexual
ambivalence becomes something like Humbert Humbert's, then, for
Scarlett can experiment with the adult roles of mother/wife (as Humbert
does with father/husband) without having to let go of the self that is
undivided in her home at Tara.

Tania Modleski says that the submerged plot of women's novels reveals an anger that's not apparent in the obvious plot: "These novels go to energetic extremes to neutralize women's anger and make masculine hostility bearable." The romance heroine's marriage, according to Modleski, equates with Frye's descent myth ("I'll die, but I'll be back") and provides the potential for revenge and power.[31] Jacques LeGoff points out that recourse to the dream or vision opens wide the gate to the popular imagination. Pagan folkloric tales of journeys to the "otherworld" were suppressed by the church because they enable "visions of the beyond."[32] Martin says "Popular formulaic narratives . . . might yield interesting information about our society if their unconscious content could be recovered."[33]

But my third reservation is that we can't be sure what happens in *any* reader's uptake of a text. Another intention I had when I began this project was to corroborate my theories by gathering reader-response accounts of what contemporary readers were getting out of various examples of the texts I'm analyzing here. But work with some other reader-response data-gathering projects changed my mind about doing my own reader-response searching. Readers *respond* as well as decode in programmed ways. I've come to believe that we can't know what readers get out of reading any more than we can understand why or in what way one person loves another. The transactions from the reader's mind to the verbalization are either too socially constructed or too imbedded in "deep structure" (as Noam Chomsky might say) to achieve dependable rendering.

So I feel that I'm left being able to explain *how* lowbrow novels work, *what* their fundamental features are, and *why* we shouldn't be so quick to pass negative judgment on them, but unable to argue just what function they serve. I am persuaded that lowbrow fiction engages a different human faculty than highbrow—call it the subconscious, the intuition, the emotion, or the id. Middlebrow perhaps engages the superego, and highbrow the ego.

This leads me to the fourth reservation: that what I am talking about is not so much literary criticism but a paradigm shift. The Gutenberg revolution, the Age of Reason, Social Darwinism are receding. It has become apparent to me that, concerns for our jobs and personal prestige aside, academics are disdainful of non-literary fiction not just because we feel that the pleasure of a really good book is so much deeper and its truths more accurate and enduring, but because we fear a revolution that will devalue our special skills.

Dinesh D'Souza expresses that fear,[34] as does Neil Postman, as does all the literature from the Frankfurt school decrying our brainwashing by the media. TV, rock music, and supermarket fiction have become the "witches" of our current hunt, things we feel beguile us into hedonism, ritualism, perversion, and anarchy. The presumed capacity of highbrow literature to give us independent strength, to pull us away from the social institutions that teach us to conform, to assuage our neediness, and to teach us to heed the intellect rather than marketplace is a mighty draw to those of us nurtured on the notion that self-control is the highest good. We have made, Terry Eagleton notwithstanding, a fetish of literary studies. We seek salvation through intellectualism. Cartesian self-control has been the creed which we believed would save us from the bootblacking factory.

At bottom we fear that when discipline and self-control lose out as prime features of what we recognize as quality, we become less than we're capable of being.[35] Still, as Freud's *Civilization and Its Discontents* indicates, we're disappointed that control over nature did not enhance happiness. Some of the dilemma comes, says Freud, because Christianity puts too low a value on the *things of this world.*[36] Some of it comes, as Scheman suggests, because we've denied the body its due.[37] Ihab Hassan says that because we repress Dionysus, or threaten the life instincts, he threatens to erupt with a vengeance.[38]

Our fear that popular cultural artifacts *create* negative values and deplete our nobler selves masks the fear that the artifacts merely reflect real selves, who might like to, say, lash out at the woman upstairs who abuses her child or have some excitement or risk in our lives more genuine than turning right on red even though we've seen the "no turn on red" sign.[39] Our other fear is that our rationality, the powers of our minds, are not capable of relieving us of the anxieties of the daily grind and that characters like Forrest Gump perhaps are.

Dickstein says that one value of popular fiction is that it accepts our dual nature, without which the individual must accept responsibility for all wrong-doing.[40] Fiedler speaks of the same dilemma: "It's profoundly disturbing that vulgar works like Griffith's and Dixon's move us beneath our consciousness, yet we cannot suppress our unconfessed ambivalence" (210). However successfully *The Assistant* examines Frank Alpine's dual nature, his circumcision does not shake off his burden of guilt. Perhaps murderous excision, ala Steven King, is required.

Civilization is being propelled in a direction that devalues the power of the highbrow novel. In an age of overpopulation and energy depletion, we suffer guilt over what we have, anxiety for what we don't. It's a world wherein it's hard to attain the feeling that we're in the right place doing the right thing, where we're not sure the guy next to us is more likely to lend a helping hand or a kick in the teeth. We're less confident than we had been in the Cartesian Age of Reason that we can use our intellects to master the urges of the soul and the requirements of society simultaneously.

Lowbrow culture can serve these anxieties better than highbrow. Take a movie like *E.T.* Here's this alien—homely and short and unable to communicate—left alone in a strange place desperate to be reunited with his culture again. "Home" is his recuperation of the divided self, a place where his body and his yearnings come together. How can he get there? Through the help of others—kids in particular. The adult community in this film only wants to ignore or analyze E.T., use or abuse someone who is "other." Adults are too self-absorbed, too busy making sure they don't fumble opportunities for advancement, but the kids are free to identify with his sense of privation.

E.T.'s bereavement in this film is our own, for, since the early stages of capitalism, especially from the fifties era of upward and outward mobility, we all lose our home, by that compunction to get beyond it. Thus alienated, we find that there's nobody there quite like us, and we long for "the blissful breast." And we all hope, like E.T., that there'll be someone who will treat us like family rather than freaks.

What this movie says, contrary to what a highbrow film would say, is that reunion with our "home" is possible only with help from others, and, even if we're not the ones to achieve the recuperation, we can get some satisfaction out of helping someone else get it. One thing that makes lowbrow literature less than insidious is that "good luck" and "bad luck" are not agentless forces in the standard plots, but *people*. Things work out well for characters who run into "good" people, not so well if they run into "bad."

Granted this is Walt Disney—well, Stephen Spielberg: apparently innocent entertainment and not at all like the kind of pulp fiction that people generally fear is debilitating "trash." I purposely addressed myself to the kind of reading that *could* make its way into high school and college English curricula—where it can be properly taught—without raising too many hackles.

What we do now by ignoring most middlebrow and virtually all lowbrow books (once students get beyond the tenth grade), is subject students to a pretty steady diet of novel-reading that emphasizes ambiguous outcomes and gives little reason to maintain hope or extend help to others. And, since I haven't even touched on the topic of their accessibility, I'll let Camille Paglia make a point for me:

> Hollywood movies of the 50's, like *The Ten Commandments* and *Ben-Hur*, with their epic clash of pagan and Judeo-Christian cultures, tell more truth about art and society than the French-infatuated ideologues who have made a travesty of the best American higher education. (29)

We don't accomplish anything when we don't reach our intended audience.

But more important than this sentimentality for a more communal and accessible world is a warning to keep abreast of the times. Highbrow culture has already been displaced as hegemonic. Though English departments across the nation may fight to salvage their Milton and Shakespeare requirements, there will a sea of students whose impatience with these relics will sink their professors into submission. And the necessity to incorporate multiethnic literature into school curricula is now leading us to embrace much folkloric literature. Learning some strategies of lowbrow and middlebrow fiction may be the best Mae West in the West. (That's a life jacket—in case you didn't catch my drift.)

NOTES

1. "Marxism and Popular Fiction: Problems and Perspectives," *Southern Review* 15 (July 1982): 228.

2. *Toward an Aesthetic of Reception*, trans. Timothy Bahti (Minneapolis: U or Minnesota P, 1982), 25.

3. "Critical Approaches toward High and Low," in Kretzoi, ed., *High and Low in American Culture* (Budapest: Loránd Eötuös U, 1986), 92.

4. Roger Chartier, "Culture as Appropriation: Popular Cultural Uses in Early Modern France," in Steven L. Kaplan, ed., *Understanding Popular Culture: Europe from the Middle Ages to the Nineteenth Century*, New Babylon Studies in the Social Sciences (Berlin, NY: Mouton, 1984), 234.

5. This a term of linguistic pragmatics; it identifies signals about meaning that derive from juxtaposition, omission, and emphasis, to name a few instances. John R. Searle, *Expression and Meaning: Studies in the Theory of*

Speech Acts (Cambridge, MA: Cambridge UP, 1979), and Mary Louise Pratt, *Toward a Speech-Act Theory of Literary Discourse* (Bloomington: U of Indiana P, 1977).

6.   *Reading the Romance* (Chapel Hill, NC: U of North Carolina P, 1984), 6.

7.   Brian Wicker, *Story-Shaped World: Fiction and Metaphysics: Some Variations on a Theme* (Notre Dame, IN: U of Notre Dame P, 1975), 12.

8.   Mickey Spillane, *One Lonely Night* (1951; New York: Signet, 1979), 102. Further quotations will be cited from this edition.

9.   Ben Ray Redman, "Decline and Fall of the Whodunit," *Saturday Review* (31 May 1952), 32.

10.   "Mickey Spillane and his Bloody Hammer," *Saturday Review* (6 November 1954), 11-12.

11.   "The Philosophy of the Beat Generation," *Esquire* (February 1958), 37.

12.   *The Theory of the Novel*, trans. Anna Bostock (Cambridge, MA: MIT P, 1971), 61.

13.   "Ninnies, Pedants, Tyrants and Other Academics," *New York Times Review of Books* (5 May 1991), 33.

14.   "The Dark and Haunted Tower of Richard Wright," in Hemenway, ed., *The Black Novelist* (Columbus, OH: Merrill, 1970), 84.

15.   *The Negro Novel in America* (New Haven, CT: Yale UP, 1965), 197.

16.   *The Novel Now* (London: Faber, 1967), 203.

17.   "The Politics of Ellison's Booker: *Invisible Man* as Symbolic History," in Hemenway, 91-92.

18.   Kostelanetz, 104 and 110.

19.   *Speech Acts: An Essay in the Philosophy of Language* (Cambridge, MA: Cambridge UP, 1969), 50 and 172.

20.   *American Social Fiction: James to Cozzens* (Edinburgh: Oliver and Boyd, 1964), 203.

21.   Max Allan Collins and James L. Traylor, *One Lonely Knight: Mickey Spillane's Mike Hammer* (Bowling Green, OH: Bowling Green UP, 1984), 37-39.

22.   LaFarge calls this explanation of "blood-lust" no excuse, for the "tried and toughened" can afford to be gentler (54).

23.   45. Instead of developing two characters to represent the "good self" and the "bad self" (as Winsor does with Amber and her lover's wife—see chapter three), Spillane presents conflicting selves in one character (as does Malamud with Frank Alpine).

24.   Like Barthes in *Mythologies*, Neil Postman expresses anxiety about the power of the image to seduce: "What worries me is that we have not yet figured out how to build defenses against the seductions of imagery." "She Wants Her TV! He Wants His Book!" *Harper's* (March 1991), 47.

25.   Christopher Norris, *Deconstruction: Theory and Practice* (London: Methuen, 1982), 48.

26. The vulnerability in Spillane, according to Sisk, arises when human affairs fall short and Utopian dreams give way to despair: the Dream Girl is fundamentally evil. "Keats' American Dream," *America* (12 March 1960), 707. Even LaFarge notes Hammer's fear that the evil ones can't be blown away (51).

27. Morris Dickstein points out that during the fifties, communism lost influence in America and became servile and manipulative. *Gates of Eden: American Culture in the Sixties* (New York: Penguin, 1977), 41.

28. Anika LeMaire, *Jacques Lacan*, trans. David Macy (London: Routledge and Kegan Paul, 1970), 188.

29. Quoted in Flynn and Schweickart, *Gender and Reading: Essays on Readings, Texts, and Contexts* (Baltimore: Johns Hopkins UP, 1986), xxiii. Sexual ambivalence is evident even in macho Mike Hammer novels. In one, he falls in love with a woman who's become female through a sex-change operation; in *One Lonely Night* Hammer takes note of a guy who "looked like a girl" who squeals with pleasure "when a girl who looked like a guy spoke" (29).

30. *"Gone with the Wind*: The Mammy of Them All," in Radford, 127-131. Another subtextual reading is Fiedler's suggestion that *GWTW* is "soft porn," for the sado-masochism which "moves us by nightmare of black insurrection." *What Was Literature?* (New York: Simon and Schuster, 1982), 195.

31. *Loving with a Vengeance*: Mass-Produced Fantasies for Women (Hamden, CT: Archon, 1982), 25, 45, and 58.

32. *Time, Work and Culture in the Middle Ages*, trans. Arthur Goldhammer (Chicago UP, 1980), 31-34.

33. Wallace Martin, *Recent Theories of Narrative* (Ithaca: Cornell UP, 1986), 24.

34. I'm alluding to his *Illiberal Education: The Politics of Law and Sex on Campus* (New York: Free, 1991).

35. Northrop Frye, *Secular Scripture: A Study in the Structure of Romance* (Cambridge, MA: Harvard UP, 1976), 25-26.

36. Trans. James Strachey (1830; New York: Norton, 1961), 192.

37. Naomi Scheman, "Though This Be Madness, Yet There Is Method in It," in *Engenderings: Constructions of Knowledge, Authority, and Privilege* (New York: Routledge, 1993), 94-96.

38. "The Dismemberment of Orpheus," *American Scholar* 32 (Summer 1963): 463-65.

39. Betty Rosenberg says that since "real life is often incredibly boring . . . women read romances when their lives lack romance." *Genreflecting: A Guide to Reading Interests in Genre Fiction* (Littleton, CO: Libraries Unlimited, 1982), 28-30.

40. *Gates of Eden*, 76.

APPENDIX

THE FIFTIES

The American fifties is an era famed for consensus, but not stupidity. With or without conscious intention, the conservatism of the fifties served the self-interest of the majority who had prospered in postwar years and were enjoying a standard of living their parents only dreamed of. What they had gained seemed worth struggling for. Convinced that they had earned their comfort and luxury through right and appropriate behavior, the public decided that prosperity might survive if no one rocked the boat. Such an assessment outlawed risk-taking.

Internationally we were content to let our success in World War II serve as the hallmark of our military superiority. Nationally we hung on nominally to New Deal philosophy, unwilling to risk the unsettling results of a true free-market economy. Domestically, we retreated to time-worn notions of sexual division and male supremacy in order to avoid real competition in the work world. Humanistically we preferred not to extend human potential.

The fifties corporation taught the "social ethic" to huge sectors of the populace. William H. Whyte, Jr., identifies these as three basic tenets of this ethic: 1) The group is the source of creativity; 2) "Belongingness" is an ultimate human need; 3) We achieve our needs through science—that is, through reason and analysis, as opposed to faith, tradition, or hard work[1] Working hard still brought industrial workers the benefits of overtime wages and corporate workers the visibility necessary for promotion. But hard work began to take second place to being cooperative, projecting the right kind of company image, and living the right kind of corporate life. Whyte points out that one couldn't even get into the white collar world, let alone advance in it, without a "normal" group-oriented personality, standards, and interests.[2]

Being indistinct was more profitable than being noticed. As a result, neither industry or the white collar world provided self-actualizing job satisfaction.[3] The pride of accomplishment and the pleasure of seeing a job completed had to be found elsewhere—in the home. In the wake of the Depression and World War II, the security and comfort of the suburban ranch house was an especially welcome human respite.[4]

Recognizing the rapid and radical changes in the work world make fifties idealization of marriage, home, and children understandable. John P. Diggins says that loneliness is a significant factor of life in postwar America.[5] Many suburbanites were living at a remove from the family and friends they grew up with. To be happy in the suburbs, they had to find in their marriages, homes, and neighborhoods satisfactory surrogates for community, identity, and productivity. In general, it was not suburbanites themselves who saw the suburban rage of the fifties as a sell-out; after all, it would take more than a few years for most people to admit to themselves that the dream they had achieved was not the panacea they thought it would be. People played the game with good will.

Those who dwell on the oppressive conformity of fifties suburbia often ignore or forget what suburbia was an alternative to. The "white collarization" of our economy meant commonplace relocation for career purposes. Where thirty years earlier most Americans grew up and worked in the communities of their birth, in the fifties, forty-two percent located elsewhere when settling into careers, and fifty-eight percent relocated two or more times in the course of that career.[6] The postwar era saw the percentage of the population living on family farms drop from forty to eight. Small-town America was on the decline.[7]

The suburbs compensated for the loss of rootedness through neighborliness. The unwritten suburban contract stipulated that one provide time for unscheduled visits, block parties, backyard barbecues, potluck suppers, carpools, child-care exchanges, and a general concern for your neighbor's welfare.[8] For the kid who had decided to leave the family farm, suburbia had the advantage over a city apartment of having some "acreage" and some distance from neighbors; for the relocated small-towner it had the simultaneous advantages of a self-contained community without a "wrong side of the tracks." For former city dwellers, suburbia provided space, both inside the house, where there was often a bedroom for each child, and outside, where children could play some place other than in the streets. And it was a relatively peaceful and cooperative environment. Whyte points out that life in city row houses was marked by competition and jealousy, while a cooperative spirit marked suburban life (337).

It's not hard to see why hundreds of thousands of Americans dreamed of owning a home in the suburbs and enjoying the benefits of suburban life. One of those benefits is the instantaneous sense of belonging that comes with owning a home. But the houses themselves—low-to-the-ground ranch styles with big picture windows and easy access to the outside, surrounded by large moat-like yards—suggest a number of contradictions. The lower structure with its turtle-shell roof is less assertive, but also less vulnerable. The picture window suggests openness, but it also helps the residents to keep an eye on what's going on out there. The enclosed, attached garage with a driveway out to the street announces that one is always ready and able to get out of there.

Their designers claimed that the one-story models marked a change in American living from formal to informal and from "interiority" to "exteriority" that emphasized convenience, naturalness, and comfort rather than elegance.[9] But the requisite well-trimmed lawn is both formal and unnatural, and the non-energy-efficient designs flaunt wealth (the lack of need to conserve on building materials, heat, and land), if not status.

Furthermore, the huge lawn provided significant framing, a large plain backdrop against which the very existence of a house is inescapable. In spite of gross similarities to its counterparts, a passer-by was afforded ample opportunity to recognize minute distinctions among suburban houses. Daniel Bell, who rejects many social criticisms laid against the fifties, argues that the purchasing power of the fifties gave people money enough to demonstrate their uniqueness.[10] Compared to a closely set row of two- or three-story city dwellings, tract homes offered both greater isolation and greater recognizability, rather than greater conformity.

The negative effects of neighborliness—the squelching of individuality and the appropriation of time—were perhaps offset by the real gains of suburban existence in the fifties. Critics tend to overlook the boredom and pettiness of small towns (*Main Street, Peyton Place*) and the squalor, crime, anonymity, and lack of privacy of urban living (*L'Assomoir, Sister Carrie, On the Waterfront, The Assistant*).

Rootless Americans of the fifties seemed willing to pay the price the suburbs exacted for "belongingness," especially because they had access to higher salaries in urban jobs and their children to good schools and cultural and athletic opportunities. If residents felt that suburbs didn't allow them opportunities for self-actualization, they could always hope it would help their kids (writer Frank O'Connor argues that the "dreams of escape" of the "submerged population," are deferred onto the children).[11]

In one sense, the rootlessness of the fifties had to be a very liberating experience, one that freed the drifters to suburbia from the ready-made definitions of self that came with being born into this or that family, or with being a doctor, a bootblack, a farmer, or offspring of the same.

But, as Erich Fromm articulates in *Escape from Freedom*, such liberation drives us to seek confinement and limits. When we have too many choices, we make significant life moves that reduce the number of choices we have to make and thus reduce the anxiety that making choices generates.[12] Newly settled suburbanites opted for the choices others had already made: They made a practice of doing what the neighbors did. They aspired to marriage, three or more children, a house with a nice big yard, and an income that afforded them the pleasures of taking a yearly trip to a national park or Disneyland, owning a family car, and generally "keeping up with the Joneses." And they expected that their conformity would provide satisfying and desirable rewards—security, comfort, friendship, sexual fulfillment, prosperity, and general good will.[13] Whether or not they fulfilled anyone's vision of happiness, these rewards were forthcoming.

Purchasing power was at an all-time high, and more and more wonderful inventions were attainable through this new power. With a free-spending attitude encouraged by big savings accounts accumulated during the war when there was nothing much to buy[14] and the new "line of credit" concept,[15] the fifties was an easy time to relish the joys of the marketplace. Americans rationalized their prodigality by spending mainly on household and family items to "strengthen the American way of life."[16] While so much was attainable that had been so recently unattainable, it was easy for Americans to ignore what analysts began seeing as an empty, stultifying life.

It's an oversimplification to attack the fifties for consumer "hoggishness" wherein all values were wholesaled by greed.[17] What was lost to the average American through urbanization, white-collarization, and cultural uprooting had to be compensated for in more than material goods. It required, in fact, a wholly revamped ethic which Whyte calls the social ethic and Elaine Tyler May "domestic containment."[18]

This containment stressed conformity and magnified the expectations of home and marriage. Diggins reports that in 1957 ninety-seven percent of people of marriageable age in America were married (213).

They also married at a younger age than previous generations, and they thought they had everything to gain by marrying. May reports that married respondents to a Kelly Longitudinal Study said they gave up "nothing" to marry and raise a family (28).

But they also expected their marriages to be satisfying in many ways. Wives expected their husbands to be "new husbands": not just beneficent providers and good role models for their children, but also satisfying lovers, active parents, and good companions. *McCall's* coined the term "togetherness" in 1954.[19] Husbands expected wives who would show the world their skills at homemaking, mothering, and socializing, and show them patience, passion, and solicitude.

While these conceptions are not a dramatic revision of previous values, the fifties stringently enforced the requirement to fulfill these images. As a result, both spouses suffered. Men had too much responsibility, according to the psychologist Maslow.[20] And women were driven to valium and psychiatrists' couches when they couldn't figure out why such satisfying and stimulating roles as motherhood and homemaking were not satisfying and stimulating to them.[21] So dominant was the notion that a woman's only happiness was to be found as a wife and mother that single women were looked upon as warped and unnatural. The authors of a book entitled *Modern Woman: The Lost Sex* even wondered if a single woman might not be unfit to teach children.[22]

Though the endless stereotyping of women as bubble-headed, overly emotional, weak, and essentially maternal seems motivated by the decade's strong family organization and its postwar sexism, certainly a good deal of it was prompted by fear that women (having proved it in the thirties and forties) were capable of stepping into any job available. The truisms that "woman's place is in the home," that motherhood is woman's ultimate satisfaction, and that any woman who didn't achieve home and family was sentenced to an unfulfilled existence were effective in discouraging women from competing in the marketplace.[23] Clark sees women in the fifties as suffering under the contradiction between self-sufficiency and ineptitude (173).

The same brainwashing techniques had been used on blacks since emancipation. These "big lies" had discouraged them from entering the competitive marketplace: that blacks are happy being told what to do, that they are by nature not very ambitious, and that they are intellectually incapable of anything above menial work.[24] That women virtually remained silent through the fifties while blacks became activists is probably because blacks were more economically deprived.

Oakley points out that the gap between black and white wages remained constant since before WWII and that no civil rights legislation had been passed since 1875 (337 and 381). Women could at least marry a higher income than they were capable of earning. Blacks needed the earning power themselves, but they couldn't get the jobs without an education that was equivalent to what whites were getting. And so they fought to defeat the old "separate but equal" ruling that had deprived them since 1875, and they fought to get into accredited universities. The 1954 Brown v. the Board of Education Supreme Court ruling required integrated schools, but its implementation was long in coming and required the persistent activism of Southern blacks.

Many whites fought to maintain traditions of racism that kept blacks "in their place"—that is, as sharecroppers and menial laborers—and out of schools, universities, stores, restaurants and social institutions that would teach blacks the skills and knowledge needed to compete with whites. The ethic that supported such discrimination bore little relationship to real motives: We tried hard to maintain that sex roles, racial capacities, and the appropriate height of the neighbor's grass were ordained by God under the general dictum that there was "a place for everything and everything in its place."

To vouchsafe God's superior position in the order of things was also a stringent requirement of the fifties—probably not so much as an article of theological faith, but as a means of testing commitment to the social ethic.[25] It seems indicative of our anxiousness on the matter that we added "under God" to the pledge of allegiance and "In God We Trust" to all our currency in this decade of America's history.[26] Perhaps because they seemed to put more trust in their own instincts and judgments than the consensus-abiding general public, atheists were judged about as dangerous in public positions as dedicated career women.

The superficiality of fifties religion is revealed in noting the things we actually did have faith in. Whyte applies the nineteenth-century term "scientism" to the general mode of belief in this decade. He observes that people were inclined to regard "experts" as the source of appropriate guidelines to follow. Dr. Spock, for example, was the expert on how to parent, replacing both the wisdom of older generations and a parent's own instincts about how to respond to a child's behavior. Kinsey taught the nation how it ought to feel about sexual behavior (407-9).

The scenario that consensus-lovers had to accept was rife with submerged anxiety, denial, falsehood and boredom, but it had its benefits. Abundance, as David Potter points out, is a force that keeps people in place.[27] But it was also inevitable that the majority's sense of "abundance" would undergo revision when it extracted too great a price in self-deception or self-denial. Oakley views Timothy Leary's "launching" of the drug culture in August of 1960 as a sign of the breakdown of the hope and contentment that buoyed America through the fifties (395, 412-13). Warren Susman warns that "the instinctual will always come back."[28]

In examining the duality of American consciousness in the fifties, Susman explains it as an "age of anxiety" wherein the fear that what has been recently gained can be easily lost transformed into a paranoia about government takeovers.[29] The McCarthy "witch hunt" provided a focus for this anxiety at the national level, as the Cold War did on a global level. From the distant perspective of the nineties, we look at McCarthyism as an historical aberration, the showpiece of a drunken megalomaniac. But the presence of a House Un-American Activities Committee (formed in the thirties), the Alien Registration Act of 1940, and the establishment of FBI security checks on all government employees in 1947 refute McCarthy's idiosyncrasy. The nation was eager for McCarthy's lurid exposés, factual or otherwise.

McCarthy's naming of Moscow-loyal infiltrators into government and cultural positions was based on scant or fabricated evidence; there is no evidence that significant atomic secrets were passed to Russian scientists or that Hollywood movies with "pro-communist themes" stimulated anti-capitalist sympathies. While it was acknowledged that American sympathizers with the communist cause did consider themselves loyal to Russian Stalinists, no sustained anti-capitalist movements surfaced.

Of course one could speculate that had we not conducted something of a purge by means of loyalty oaths and anti-communist propagandizing, communist sympathizing might have become more flagrant and influential. Or it might have led to reformed principles of democracy. For example, openness might have led to the sharing of nuclear information among scientists across national boundaries—a move strongly urged by many in the scientific community who thought that scientific knowledge is not a national property and that the cause of nuclear control could be better served by mutual cooperation. But, perhaps because of a "post-Depression mentality" (affluence ruins character; people become overly competitive, anxious about failure), we clung fiercely to what we had in our own possession like a child afraid that what we let out of our grasp we'd never get back.[30]

Americans gained something from seeing Russia and communism as targets of suspicion—a focus for their anxiety that whatever bounty they were enjoying would somehow surely be usurped from them. As a nation we had never had it as good as we did in the fifties, and many of those who were enjoying the forty percent increase in spending power over 1929[31] had been alive through the Depression and had seen how easy it is for plenty to become ashes, how difficult to recover what has disintegrated.

In addition, the "Red Scare" provided Americans with an argument that they had to defend their system of free enterprise and personal initiative against less materially successful nations jealous of America's bounty. Nixon, in his famous "kitchen debate," proudly pointed out to Nikita Khrushchev the labor-saving and convenience appliances that he assumed housewives all over the world coveted.[32]

And under that mentality middle-class Americans began to question New Deal policies and Keynesian economic practices. While they basked in the comfort of a prosperity engineered through compromises of the free market system—deficit spending, artificial price supports, and "creeping socialism"—there was little resistance to such legislation as long as those compromises were increasing the spending power of the majority.[33]

When supportive taxes threatened to decrease spendable income, there was pressure to put the brakes on policies that would lead America into a socialized system. Oakley says that the populace persuaded themselves that no further programs were required to alleviate the plight of the poor; poverty would cure itself (218). Americans were undoubtedly aware that pushing the concept of equal opportunity to its logical ends would require providing equal opportunities for racial minorities and hasten desegregation in schools and universities, in business and industry, in public places and private professions. The stalemate in social action was abetted by a Democratic Congress and a Republican administration that managed to keep each other from doing much that was drastic.

What Americans really wanted was a tax-free way to preserve the notion that we were a land of equal and endless opportunity. The Truman administration continued to support New Deal legislation with the Full Employment Act (1946), the Atomic Energy Act (1946), and the National Security Council system of protections. Truman presented a "fair deal" package to Congress in 1949 that included increased social security benefits and a minimum wage.

But the Taft-Hartley Act of 1947 jeopardized the power of unions by sanctioning government action against strikes (supporting Truman's own seizing of the railroads during the strike of 1946). Oakley says that through the fifties the Department of Justice was "not in a trust-busting mood" (233). Diggins points out that Eisenhower's cabinet was composed of millionaires who adopted the philosophy that what was good for General Motors was good for the nation (130). Although Ike did little to undo New Deal policies already in practice, his campaign promise and chief goal in office was a balanced budget—a signal that, essentially, "the New Deal stopped here." His supporters, according to Oakley, wanted to end the drift towards socialism (139).

On a tour of Indochina, Eisenhower was appalled at the deep and widespread poverty he saw, and afterwards undertook to inaugurate programs for Third World relief (which Congress rejected). Yet, like many Americans at the time, he did not acknowledge the parallel in our own country.[34]

Our success in World War II and our prosperity afterwards left the U.S. in another dualistic predicament. We had developed a paternalistic sense of our role in global relations (the Marshall Plan and the policy of communist containment) at the same time that we feared to upset present tranquility by asserting that paternalism.

Because we had played a waiting game before entering a war which clearly could have benefited earlier from U.S. personnel and materiel, and then had come in as nonaggressive victims of the Pearl Harbor attack, we felt that we fought with God on our side. Being the first to have nuclear weapons and then having the guts to use them to stun the Japanese added muscle to this moralism.

We saw ourselves as a nation to be reckoned with, not merely because we were prosperous and powerful, but also because we used our might judiciously. We believed that war effort, when applied for the sake of world relief, was justified and noble.[35] On the other hand, the bravado of these convictions is revealed by our military tentativeness throughout the decade (in Egypt and Hungary, for example), by our willingness to let McCarthy cast communism as an insidious monster, and by our pervasive fear of nuclear holocaust. Both Truman's and Eisenhower's policies in Korea, the Mideast, China, and Indochina upheld the fine impression that we were caretakers of the *right* way of life who entered combat only to rescue the oppressed and to promote democracy.

But our support of Syngman Rhee's Korean nationalist regime was motivated not by the people's choice, but by Rhee's unwillingness to cede power to Chinese communists. We were similarly inconsistent in our support of Nationalist Chinese leader Chiang Kai-shek despite the fact that Mao's takeover had the overwhelming support of the populace.

And in Indochina, we indefinitely postponed elections dictated by the Geneva Conference that would surely have given Ho Chi Minh control of all of Vietnam. U.S. policy was against any revolutionary regime that might strengthen Moscow's grip on the world and for any ruling power—no matter how totalitarian or repressive—that opposed communism. Diggins criticizes our fifties foreign policy for supporting tyrannical leaders like Syngman Rhee and Diem and then failing to assist a genuine anti-communist popular uprising in Hungary in 1956, because we feared nuclear retaliation.[36] Oakley believes that Eisenhower misread Diem's position because he was too eager to believe he was fighting communist aggression (393).

Even so, we were unwilling to commit to full military confrontation. The Marshall Plan prescribed that we abandon Quemoy and Matsu to fate in spite of popular support for their defense—if a *Collier's* article can be taken as an indication of that. Adm. Charles M. Cooke, USN (ret.), wrote for this magazine:

> [H]alfway around the globe, Communism is in action in the old way. . . . For reasons not always clear to the American people, the defense of Quemoy and Matsu . . . has taken on a crucial urgency.[37]

Still free from Red Chinese domination, the islands were harassed by sporadic attacks from the mainland, but the U.S. determined that these islands were useless as military bases, and their defense would leave us unprepared for trouble arising in more critical locales.

Another example of our military timidity occurred when Nasser nationalized the Suez Canal and prevented Israeli ships from passing. France and Britain declared readiness for military confrontation to protect their oil supplies, but the United States adopted a wait-and-see policy, apparently afraid that its entry into armed confrontation would compel Russia to assist Nasser and that Russia's military preparedness would outshine ours.[38] Of course it's easy to rationalize that our reluctance to enter into combat showed our sanity, humanity and control, but Diggins charges that the United States was hamstrung both by its possession of nuclear superiority and its insecurity about Russia's power (346).

Our growing awareness of the effects of nuclear fallout (evidence existed of genetic defects in both humans and livestock and of contaminated air and soil far outside the boundaries of the bomb's explosive radius) prompted some of this caution, as did the awareness that a nuclear war would be a "no-win" war. Throughout the fifties the increase in destructive capacity of bombs and the growing number of nations who had developed usable nuclear weapons augmented these fears.

We were in a bind. As the nation with the greatest nuclear capability and one dedicated to making the world safe for democracy, it behooved us not to use them. But we could not *not* develop nuclear weapons because other countries—and surely Russia among them—were developing them. Through his two administrations Eisenhower quadrupled the defense budget, and the bulk of that commitment was to the development of nuclear weaponry.[39] Thus we became the chief stockholders of a commodity of questionable market value, and we had to conduct business as usual for fear that other shareholders would cash in or engage in hostile takeover. We had to brandish our nuclear superiority but we dared not use it.

The Red Scare, the "domino effect," world domination, and communist aggression were watchwords the nation used to guide its foreign policy through the fifties. We greeted every instance of aggression—North Korea's attack of the 38th parallel, Nasser's seizing of the Canal, China's attack on Quemoy and Matsu, the Cuban revolution—as proof that Moscow was engineering yet another phase of its plan to take over the world.

Diggins believes that throughout this decade Russia, economically, scientifically, and materially ill-equipped to match us missile for missile, gained valuable "catch-up time" from U.S. paranoia. Our nuclear capacity, by Diggins's estimation, was ten times greater than Russia's through most of the decade.[40] Oakley says that Russia was more missile-ready than we in 1955 (343), but concedes that Russia's furor over our U-2 spy missions may show their desire to prevent us from discovering their unpreparedness (387-89).

We accepted with little proof the notion that Russia was amassing a greater stockpile of nuclear arms than we had, that they were developing missiles superior to our own remarkable ICBMs, that they had a well-maintained and supplied standing army, that Red China and Soviet Russia were allies sworn to assist each other against European or American aggression, and that they were bent on world domination. And we allowed this fear to dominate both our foreign and domestic policy.

It's not hard to see a consistent theme running through many aspects of fifties life: the handmaiden of *having* is the fear of losing. More than wallowing in hoggish materialism in the fifties, Americans were stultified by it. We were owned by our prosperity. "What we came to see," writes John Mander, "was that the society our prophetic ancestors so passionately assailed was, indeed, the worst of all possible systems—with the exception, of course, of all others."[41]

NOTES

1. Whyte sees the "social ethic" as the pervasive philosophy of the fifties. *The Organization Man* (Garden City, NY: Doubleday, 1956), 7-8.

2. 190-235. Whyte sees the great increase in the use of personality tests for prospective employees (especially as they came to replace aptitude tests) as a sign that companies were interested in loyalty above any other factor. He cites *The Caine Mutiny* as evidence that the ethic of the fifties was to never buck the system (272).

3. Whyte believes that people need "whole jobs" for self-respect (445). Jackson Lears describes the modern corporation as a "total institution" that erases selfhood. "A Matter of Taste: Corporate Cultural Hegemony in a Mass-Consumption Society," in Lary May, *Recasting America: Culture and Politics in the Age of the Cold War* (Chicago: U of Chicago P, 1989), 45.

4. Elaine May cites C. W. Clark on the "reckless psychological state" after great disasters; *Homeward Bound: American Families in the Cold War Era (New York: Basic, 1988)*, 92.

5. *The Proud Decade: America in War and Peace, 1941-1960* (New York: Norton, 1988), 27.

6. Whyte, 304. Whyte says that all "organization men" had "left home."

7. Diggins, 323.

8. See E. May, 24, and Whyte, 314 and 317. Whyte calls suburbs "hotbeds of participation" and cites ads enticing buyers to the suburbs because they're welcoming and friendly.

9. Clifford E. Clark, "Ranch-House Suburbia: Ideals and Realities," in L. May, 174.

10. *The End of Ideology* (New York: Free, 1960), 34.

11. *The Lonely Voice: A Study of the Short Story* (Cleveland: World, 1963).

12. (New York: Rinehart, 1941), 123-28.

13. Clark, 189.

14. J. Ronald Oakley says Americans had saved $150 billion during the war and that through the decade per capita income rose by 48%. *God's Country: America in the Fifties* (1968; New York: Dembner, 1990), 228-31.

15. Sears Roebuck had 10 million credit accounts in 1960. Diggins, 187.

16. E. May, 166.

17. Oakley quotes William V. Shannon, who accused the fifties' populace of "self-satisfaction and gross materialism" evident from their "grunt of purest hoggishness." *American Scholar* (30 Sept 1962), 176.

18. According to the philosophy of "domestic containment," discontent disappears when we adapt to conditions that exist instead of seeking to alter those conditions through political or other resistance (E. May 204-10).

19. Oakley, 291.

20. Diggins, 216.

21. E. May, 14. See also Betty Friedan, *The Feminine Mystique* (New York: Dell, 1963), 58-61.

22. Both Oakley and Diggins claim that this book by Marynia Farnham and Ferdinand Lundberg, published in 1946, influenced fifties thinking about women (293, 214).

23. Oakley is one who discusses how the "big lie" was used as never before to obscure the real truth about women (293).

24. Strom Thurmond used another form of the "big lie" when he urged voters to: "Preserve segregation for the sake of 'community'" (Diggins 104).

25. See Whyte, 407-9, and Oakley, 324.

26. Oakley, 185.

27. *People of Plenty: Economic Abundance and the American Character* (Chicago: U of Chicago P, 1965), 110.

28. "Did Success Spoil the United States? Dual Representations in Postwar America"; in L. May, 30-31.

29. In Lary May, 19-23.

30. Potter, 252.

31. Diggins, 35.

32. E. May, 164.

33. According to Diggins, twenty percent of Americans lived at a yearly income level of less than $2000 through the fifties (340).

34. Diggins, 307.

35. Oakley, 318.

36. John P. Diggins, *The Proud Decades: America in War and in Peace, 1941-1960* (New York: Norton, 1988), 301-10.

37. In "Quemoy: The Immediate Threat to Peace" (14 October 1955), 71.

38. Oakley, 222-23.

39. Diggins, 346.

40. This conclusion is based partly on Diggins' assessment of the vast superiority of our missiles (146).

41. "In Defense of the Fifties," *Commentary* (September 1969), 67.

BIBLIOGRAPHY

PRIMARY SOURCES

Auchincloss, Louis. *The Great World and Timothy Holt*. Boston: Houghton, 1956.

Bassing, Eileen. *Home Before Dark*. New York: Random, 1957.

Beach, Edward L. *Run Silent, Run Deep*. New York: Pocket, 1956.

Bellow, Saul. *Henderson the Rain King*. New York: Avon, 1958.

Defoe, Daniel. *Robinson Crusoe*. Chicago: Scott Foresman, 1951.

Ellison, Ralph. *Invisible Man*. 1952. New York: Vintage, 1972.

Fine, Anne. *Alias Madame Doubtfire*. 1988. New York: Bantam, 1993.

Grisham, John. *The Firm*. 1991. New York: Dell, 1992.

Hawkes, John. *The Cannibal*. 1949. New York: Little, 1968.

Hemingway, Ernest. *Across the River and into the Trees*. New York: Scribner, 1950.

Hersey, John. *The War Lover*. New York: Knopf, 1959.

Howe, Helen. *The Circle of the Day*. New York: Simon and Schuster, 1950.

Huie, Bradford. *The Execution of Private Slovik*. New York: Dell, 1954.

Humphrey, William. *Home from the Hill*. New York: Knopf, 1957.

Jones, James. *From Here to Eternity*. New York: Signet, 1951.

Kauffmann, Lane. *Six Weeks in March*. New York: Avon, 1956.

Kerouac, Jack. *On the Road*. 1957. London: Deutsch, 1968.

Kotzwinkle, William. *E.T. The Extraterrestrial in His Adventure on Earth*. Based on a Screenplay by M. Mathison. New York: Berkley, 1982.

McCarthy, Mary. *The Group*. 1954. New York: Signet, 1963.

Mailer, Norman. *The Naked and the Dead*. New York: Rinehart, 1948.

Malamud, Bernard. *The Assistant*. 1957. New York: Avon, 1980.

Metalious, Grace. *Peyton Place*. 1956. New York: Pocket, 1965.

Nabokov, Vladimir. *Lolita*. 1955. Greenwich, CT: Fawcett, 1958.

O'Connor, Flannery. *Wise Blood.* New York: Harcourt, 1952.

O'Hara, John. *Ten North Frederick.* New York: Bantam, 1955.

Purdy, James. *Malcolm.* New York: Farrar, 1959.

Rand, Ayn. *Atlas Shrugged.* New York: Signet, 1957.

Richardson, Samuel. *Clarissa, or The History of a Young Lady.* 4 vols. 1747. Everyman's Library. London: J. M. Dent, 1932.

– – –. *Pamela, or Virtue Rewarded.* 4 vols. 1740. Stratford-on-Avon: Shakespeare Head P, 1929.

Salinger, J.D. *The Catcher in the Rye.* 1951. Toronto: Bantam, 1964.

Slaughter, Frank. *The Healer.* New York: Pocket, 1955.

Spillane, Mickey. *One Lonely Night.* 1951. New York: Signet, 1979.

Styron, William. *Lie Down in Darkness.* New York: Viking, 1957.

– – –. *The Long March.* New York: Random, 1952.

Uris, Leon. *Battle Cry.* New York: Bantam, 1953.

– – –. *Exodus.* New York: Bantam, 1958.

Waller, Robert James. *The Bridges of Madison County.* New York: Warner, 1992.

Wilson, Sloan. *The Man in the Gray Flannel Suit.* New York: Pocket, 1956.

Winsor, Kathleen. *Forever Amber.* New York: Macmillan, 1945.

Wormser, Anne. *Lonesome Road. Redbook* November 1953, 102+.

Wouk, Herman. *The Caine Mutiny.* 1951. New York: Pocket, 1973.

Wright, Richard. *The Outsider.* New York: Harper and Row, 1953.

SECONDARY SOURCES

Adams, Richard P. "A Second Look at *From Here to Eternity.*" *College English* January 1956: 205-10.

Adorno, Theodor W. and Max Horkheimer. "The Culture Industry: Enlightenment or Mass Deception." In *Dialectic of the Enlightenment.* Trans. John Cumming. New York: Continuum, 1986.

Aichinger, Peter. *The American Soldier in Fiction, 1880-1963: A History of Attitudes toward Warfare and the Military Establishment.* Ames: Iowa State UP, 1975.

Aldridge, J.W. Review of *Lie Down in Darkness* by William Styron. *New York Times* 9 September 1951: 5.

Allsop, Kenneth. *The Angry Decade: A Survey of the Cultural Revolution of the 1950s.* London: P. Owen, 1964.

Alter, Richard. *After the Tradition: Essays on Modern Jewish Writing.* New York: Dutton, 1969.

Altieri, Charles. "An Idea and Ideal of a Literary Canon." *Critical Inquiry* 10.1 (1983): 37-60.

Armstrong, Thomas W. "Reader, Critic, and the Form of John Hawkes's *The Cannibal.*" *Boundary 2* 5 (1977): 829-44.

Bakhtin, Mikhail. *Rabelais and His World.* Trans. Helene Iswolsky. Cambridge, MA: MIT P, 1968.

Balakian, Nona and Charles Simmons. *The Creative Present: Notes on Contemporary American Fiction.* Garden City, NY: Doubleday, 1962.

Barr, Donald. "Ah Buddy: Salinger." In Balakian and Simmons, 25-62.

Barthes, Roland. *Image, Music, Text.* Trans. Stephen Heath. New York: Hill, 1977.

– – –. *Mythologies.* Trans. Annette Lavers. 1957. New York: Hill, 1972.

– – –. *The Pleasure of the Text.* Trans. Richard Miller. 1973. New York: Hill, 1975.

Baumbach, Jonathan. *The Landscape of Nightmare: Studies in the Contemporary American Novel.* New York: New York UP, 1965.

Bawer, Bruce. *Diminishing Fictions: Essays on the Modern American Novel and Its Critics.* St. Paul, MN: Graywolf, 1988.

Baym, Nina. *Novels, Readers, and Reviewers: Responses to Fiction in Antebellum America.* Ithaca: Cornell UP, 1984.

Bell, Daniel. *The End of Ideology: On the Exhaustion of Political Ideas in the Fifties.* New York: Free, 1960.

Bennett, Tony. "Marxism and Popular Fiction: Problems and Perspectives." *Southern Review* 15 (1982): 218-233. Also in Humm, 237-65.

Bergson, Henri. *Laughter: An Essay on the Meaning of the Comic.* Trans. C. Brereton and F. Rothwell. 1911. New York: Macmillan, 1928.

Bettelheim, Bruno. *The Uses of Enchantment: The Meaning and Importance of Fairy Tales.* New York: Knopf, 1976.

Bone, Robert. *The Negro Novel in America.* New Haven, CT: Yale UP, 1965.

Booth, Wayne C. *Modern Dogma and the Rhetoric of Assent.* 1963. Chicago: U of Chicago P, 1974.

– – –. "The Self-Conscious Narrator in Prose Fiction before *Tristram Shandy.*" *PMLA* 67 (1952), 163-185.

Brantlinger, Patrick. *Bread and Circuses: Theories of Mass Culture as Social Decay.* 1983. Ithaca: Cornell UP, 1985.

Browne, Ray B., and Marshall W. Fishwick. *The Hero in Transition.* Bowling Green, OH: Bowling Green State UP, 1983.

Bryant, Jerry. *The Open Decision*. New York: Free, 1970.

Bullock, F. H. Review of *Circle of the Day*, by Helen Howe. *New York Herald Tribune* 21 May 1950: 4.

Burgess, Anthony. *The Novel Now: A Student's Guide to Contemporary Fiction*. London: Faber, 1967.

Busch, Frederick. *Hawkes: A Guide to His Fictions*. Syracuse: Syracuse UP, 1973.

Calmer, Ned. "The Real Enemy Is Hard to Find." Review of *From Here to Eternity*. *Saturday Review of Literature* 24 February 1951: 11-12.

Calvino, Italo. *Uses of Literature*. Trans. Patrick Creagh. San Diego: Harcourt, 1986.

Carmichael, Joel. Review of *Exodus*, by Leon Uris. *Midstream* Autumn 1961: 86-89.

Cawelti, John G. *Adventure, Mystery, and Romance: Formula Stories as Art and Popular Culture*. Chicago: U of Chicago P, 1976.

Chamberlain, John. "The Conservative Miss McCarthy." *National Review* 22 October 1963: 353-55.

– – –. "The Novels of Mary McCarthy." In Balakian and Simmons, 231-256.

Chartier, Roger. "Culture as Appropriation: Popular Cultural Uses in Early Modern France." In Kaplan 229-53.

Clark, Clifford E. "Ranch-House Suburbia: Ideals and Realities." In L. May 171-91.

Clayton, John Jacob. *Saul Bellow: In Defense of Man*. Bloomington: Indiana UP, 1968.

Coleman, S.H. Review of *The Cannibal*, by John Hawkes. *Chicago Review* 4 (Winter 1950): 44-45.

Collins, Max Allan, and James L. Traylor. *One Lonely Knight: Mickey Spillane's Mike Hammer*. Bowling Green, OH: Bowling Green State UP, 1984.

Conley, Tom. Foreword. *Portrait of the King*, by Louis Marin. Trans. Martha M. Houle. Theory and History of Literature 57. Minneapolis: U of Minnesota P, 1988: vi-xvii.

Cooke, Adm. Charles M., USN (ret.). "Quemoy: The Immediate Threat to Peace." *Collier's* 14 October 1955: 70-76.

Coxe, Louis O. Review of *Man in the Gray Flannel Suit*, by Sloan Wilson. *Yale Review* 45 (1955): 154-60.

Cranston, Maurice. Review of *The Cannibal*, by John Hawkes. *London Magazine* February 1969: 95-96.

Davis, Robert Gorham. "The American Individualist Tradition in Bellow and Styron." In Balakian and Simmons, 109-142.

– – –. Review of *Ten North Frederick*, by John O'Hara. *New York Times Review of Books.* 27 November 1955: 1.

DeMott, Benjamin. "Polls, Presidents, and Perceptions." *Harper's* October 1963: 98+.

Dempsey, David. Review of *From Here to Eternity*, by James Jones. *New York Times Review of Books* 25 February 1951: 5.

Derrida, Jacques. "Signature, Event, Context." *Glyph I*. Johns Hopkins Textual Studies. Baltimore: Johns Hopkins UP, 1977: 172-79.

DeVoto, Bernard. "Dull Novels Make Dull Reading." *Harper's* June 1951: 67-70.

Dickstein, Morris. *Gates of Eden: American Culture in the Sixties.* 1977. New York: Basic, 1989.

– – –. "Popular Fiction and Critical Values: The Novel as a Challenge to Literary History." *Reconstructing American Literary History.* Sacvani Bercovitch, ed. Harvard Studies in English 13. Cambridge, MA: Harvard UP, 1986: 29-66.

Diggins, John P. *The Proud Decades: America in War and in Peace, 1941-1960.* New York: Norton, 1988.

Dolan, Paul J. *Of War and War's Alarms: Fiction and Politics in the Modern World.* New York: Free, 1976.

Dollimore, Jonathan. "The Challenge of Sexuality." In Sinfield, 51-85.

Douglas, Ann. *The Feminization of American Culture.* New York: Knopf, 1977.

D'Souza, Dinesh. "Illiberal Education." *Atlantic* March 1991: 51+. See also D'Souza's book *Illiberal Education: The Politics of Law and Sex on Campus.* New York: Free, 1991.

Ducharme, Robert. *Art and Idea in the Novels of Bernard Malamud.* The Hague: Mouton, 1974.

Eagleton, Terry. *Literary Theory: An Introduction.* Minneapolis: U of Minnesota P, 1983.

Eaton, Marcia M. *Aesthetics and the Good Life.* Rutherford, NJ: Associated UP, 1989.

– – –. *Art and Nonart: Reflections on an Orange Crate and a Moose Call.* Rutherford, NJ: Farleigh Dickinson UP, 1983.

Eco, Umberto. *The Role of the Reader: Explorations in the Semiotics of Texts.* 1979. Bloomington: Indiana UP, 1984.

Elson, Ruth Miller. *Myths and Mores in American Best Sellers.* New York: Garland, 1985.

Farrell, Paul V. "U.S. Marines." Review of *Battle Cry*, by Leon Uris. *Commonweal* 8 May 1953: 128-129.

Federmayer, Éva. "Critical Approaches toward High and Low." In Kretzoi 87-94.

Feld, Rose. "Stepping Out of Army Uniform into That of the Junior Executive." *New York Herald Tribune* 17 July 1955, sec. 6: 1.

Fiedler, Leslie. *What Was Literature? Class Culture and Mass Society.* New York: Simon and Schuster, 1982.

Flynn, Elizabeth and Patricinio Schweickart, eds. *Gender and Reading: Essays on Readings, Texts, and Contexts.* Baltimore: Johns Hopkins UP, 1986.

Foell, Earl W. "Travails and Travels of a Commuter." Review of *Man in the Gray Flannel Suit,* by Sloan Wilson. *Christian Science Monitor* 21 July 1955, sec. 2: 11.

French, Warren. "The Quaking World of James Purdy." *Essays in Modern American Literature.* Eds. R.E. Langford, G. Owen, and W.E. Taylor. DeLond, FL: Stetson UP, 1960.

Freud, Sigmund. *Civilization and Its Discontents.* Trans. James Strachey. 1930. New York: Norton, 1961.

Friedan, Betty. *The Feminine Mystique.* New York: Dell, 1963.

Friedrich, Otto. "Farewell to Peyton Place." *Esquire* December 1971: 306-25.

Fromm, Erich. *Escape from Freedom.* 1941. New York: Farrar, 1960.

Frye, Joanna. *Living Stories/Telling Lives: Women and the Novel in Contemporary Experience.* Ann Arbor: U of Michigan P, 1986.

Frye, Northrop. *The Educated Imagination.* Bloomington: Indiana UP, 1964.

– – –. *The Secular Scripture: A Study of the Structure of Romance.* Cambridge, MA: Harvard UP, 1976.

Gans, Herbert. *Popular Culture and High Culture: An Analysis and Evaluation of Taste.* New York: Basic, 1974.

Gardiner, H.C. Review of *The Group,* by Mary McCarthy. *America* 21 September 1963, 317.

Gedin, Per. *Literature in the Market Place.* Trans. George Bisset. 1975. Woodstock, NY: Overlook, 1977.

Geertz, Clifford. *The Interpretation of Cultures.* New York: Basic, 1973.

Geismar, Maxwell. *American Moderns from Rebellion to Conformity.* New York: Hill and Wang, 1958.

– – –. Review of *Lie Down in Darkness,* by William Styron. *Saturday Review of Literature* 15 September 1951: 12.

Giles, James R. *James Jones.* Twayne Author Series. Boston: Holt, 1981.

Girvin, Florence. Review of *Home Before Dark,* by Eileen Bassing. *New York Herald Tribune* 13 January 1957: 4.

Gombrich, E.H. *Art and Illusion.* London: Phaidon, 1963.

Goodman, Nelson. *Language of Art: An Approach to a Theory of Symbols.* Indianapolis: Hackett, 1976.

Graham, John. "John Hawkes on His Novels: An Interview with John Graham." *Massachusetts Review* 7 (Summer 1966): 449-461.

Green, Martin. "The Morality of *Lolita.*" *Kenyon Review* 28 (1966): 352-77.

Greenberg, Clement. "Avant-Garde and Kitsch." In Rosenberg and White, *Mass Culture,* 98-107.

Greiner, Donald J. *Comic Terror: The Novels of John Hawkes.* Memphis: Memphis State UP, 1975.

Guerard, Albert J. Introduction to *The Cannibal,* by John Hawkes: vii-xiv. New York: Little, 1963.

– – –. "The Prose Style of John Hawkes." *Critique* 6.2 (1965): 19-29.

Habermas, Jürgen. *Communication and the Evolution of Society.* Trans. Thomas McCarthy. Boston: Beacon, 1979.

Halberstam, David. *The Fifties.* New York: Villard Books, 1993.

Halpin, Lee S. "American Liberalism, Literature, and World War II." *Minnesota Review* 3 (Winter 1963): 179-92.

Hart, James. *The Popular Book: A History of America's Literary Tastes.* 1950. Westport, CT: Greenwood, 1976.

Hassan, Ihab. "Dismemberment of Orpheus: Reflections on Modern Culture, Language, and Literature." *American Scholar* 32 (1963): 463-84.

– – –. "The Novels of Outrage: A Minority Voice in Postwar American Fiction." *American Scholar* 34 (1965): 239-53.

– – –. *Radical Innocence: Studies in the Contemporary American Novel.* Princeton, NJ: Princeton UP, 1961.

Hemenway, Robert, ed. *The Black Novelist.* Columbus, OH: Merrill, 1970.

Herr, Paul. "The Small, Sad World of James Purdy." *Chicago Review* 14.3 (1960): 19-25.

Hicks, Granville. Review of *The Group,* by Mary McCarthy. *Saturday Review* 31 August 1963: 19.

Hilfer, Tony. *The Crime Novel: A Deviant Genre.* Austin: U of Texas P, 1990.

Hinckley, Karen, and Barbara Hinckley. *American Best Sellers: A Reader's Guide to Popular Fiction.* Bloomington: Indiana UP, 1989.

Hoffman, D.G. *Form and Fable in American Fiction.* New York: Oxford UP, 1961.

Hoffman, Frederick J. *The Modern Novel in America, 1900-1950.* Twentieth Century Literature in America. Chicago: Henry Regnery, 1951.

Holmes, John Clellon. "The Philosophy of the Best Generation." *Esquire* February 1958: 35-38.

Hubbard, Rita C. "The Changing-Unchanging Heroines and Heroes of Harlequin Romances 1950-1979." In Browne and Fishwick, 171-179.

Hughes, Daniel J. "Reality and the Hero: *Lolita* and *Henderson the Rain King.*" *Modern Fiction Studies* 6 (1960-61): 345-64.

– – –. "Character in Contemporary Fiction." *Massachusetts Review* 3.4 (1962): 788-95.

Humm, Peter, Paul Stigart, and Peter Widdowson, eds. *Popular Fiction: Essays in Literature and History.* London: Methuen, 1986.

Iser, Wolfgang. *The Implied Reader: Patterns of Communication in Prose Fiction from Bunyan to Beckett.* Baltimore: Johns Hopkins UP, 1974.

James, William. *The Varieties of Religious Experience.* 1902. New Hyde Park, NY: University Books, 1963.

Jameson, Frederic. "Reification and Utopia in Mass Culture." *Social Text* 1 (1979): 130-148.

Janeway, Elizabeth. Review of *Circle of the Day,* by Helen Howe. *Saturday Review* 20 June 1950: 33.

Jauss, Hans Robert. *Toward an Aesthetic of Reception.* Trans. Timothy Bahti. Theory and History of Literature 2. Minneapolis: U of Minnesota P, 1982.

Jensen, Margaret Ann. *Love's $weet Return: The Harlequin Story.* Toronto: Women's, 1984.

Jones, Ernest. *Hamlet and Oedipus.* Garden City, NY: Doubleday, 1954.

– – –. "Minority Report." Review of *From Here to Eternity,* by James Jones. *Nation* 17 March 1951: 254-55.

Jones, Peter G. *War and the Novelist: Appraising the American War Novel.* Columbia, MO: U of Missouri P, 1976.

Josipovici, G.D. "*Lolita*: Parody and the Pursuit of Beauty." *Critical Quarterly* 6.1 (1964): 35-48.

Kaplan, Steven L., ed. *Understanding Popular Culture: Europe from the Middle Ages to the Nineteenth Century.* New Babylon Studies in the Social Sciences. Berlin, NY: Mouton, 1984.

Karl, Frederich R. *American Fictions 1940-1980: A Comprehensive History and Critical Evaluation.* New York: Harper and Row, 1983.

Kauffman, Stanley. Review of *The Group*, by Mary McCarthy. *New Republic* 31 August 1963: 25.

Kelly, James. "Captive of the 5:31." Review of *Man in the Gray Flannel Suit*, by Sloan Wilson. *Saturday Review* 23 July 1955: 8-9.

Kent, Thomas. *Interpretation and Genre: The Role of Generic Perceptions in the Study of Narrative Texts.* London: Associated UP, 1986.

Kermode, Frank. *Sense of an Ending.* 1967. New York: Oxford UP, 1977.

Klein, Alexander. "The Merely New." *New Republic* 27 March 1950: 20.

Klein, Marcus. "A Discipline of Nobility." *Kenyon Review* 25 (1962): 203-32.

Kostelanetz, Richard. The Politics of Ellison's Booker: *Invisible Man* as Symbolic History." Hemenway 88-110. Reprinted from *Chicago Review* 19.2 (1967): 5-26.

Kretzoi, Charlotte, ed. *High and Low in American Culture.* Budapest: Loránd Eötuös UP, 1986.

LaFarge, Christopher. "Mickey Spillane and his Bloody Hammer." *Saturday Review* 6 November 1954: 11+.

Laing, R.D. *The Divided Self.* New York: Pantheon, 1960.

Lardner, John. "Anatomy of the Regular Army." Review of *From Here to Eternity.* *New Yorker* 10 March 1951: 117-19.

Lears, Jackson. "A Matter of Taste: Corporate Cultural Hegemony in a Mass-Consumption Society." In L. May 38-57.

LeGoff, Jacques. "Journeys to the Nether World." In Kaplan, 19-33.

LeMaire, Anika. *Jacques Lacan.* Trans. David Macy. London: Routledge and Kegan Paul, 1970.

Lerman, Leo. Review of *Circle of the Day*, by Helen Howe. *New York Times Review of Books* 28 May 1950: 8.

Levine, Lawrence. *Highbrow/Lowbrow: The Emergence of Cultural Hierarchy in America.* Cambridge, MA: Harvard UP, 1988.

Lévi-Strauss, Claude. *The Raw and the Cooked.* Trans. John Weightman and Doreen Weightman. New York: Harper and Row, 1969.

– – –. *The Savage Mind.* 1962. London: Weidenfeld and Nicholson, 1966.

– – –. *Structural Anthropology.* Trans. Claire Jacobson and Brooke Grundfest Schoepf. 1963. Garden City, NY: Doubleday, 1967.

Lewin, Martin. Review of *The Healer*, by Frank Slaughter. *Saturday Review* 12 March 1955, 44.

Lewis, C.S. *Rehabilitation and Other Essays.* London: Oxford UP, 1939.

Long, Elizabeth. *The American Dream and the Popular Novel.* New York: Routledge and Kegan Paul, 1985.

Lovell, Terry. *Consuming Fictions*. London: Verso, 1987.

Lukács, Georg. *The Theory of the Novel: A Historico-Philosophical Essay on the Forms of Great Epic Literature*. 1920. Trans. Anna Bostock. Cambridge, MA: MIT P, 1971.

Lukacs, John. *A New History of the Cold War*. 3rd ed. Garden City, NY: Anchor, 1966.

Lyotard, Jean-François. *The Post-Modern Condition: A Report on Knowledge*. Trans. Geoff Bennington and Brian Massumi. Theory and History of Literature 10. 1979. Minneapolis: U of Minnesota P, 1984.

McDonald, Dwight. *Against the American Grain*. 1952. New York: Random, 1962.

McNulty, J. Review of *Man in the Gray Flannel Suit*, by Sloan Wilson. *New York Times Review of Books* 17 July 1955: 18.

Magid, Nora. "The Gray Flannel Soul." *New Republic* 8 August 1955: 19-20.

Malinowski, Bronislaw. *Sex, Culture, and Myth*. London: Hart-Davis, 1963.

Mandel, Siegfried. Review of *Home Before Dark*, by Eileen Bassing. *Saturday Review* 26 January 1957: 32.

Marin, Louis. *Portrait of the King*. Trans. Martha M. Houle. Theory and History of Literature 57. Minneapolis: U of Minnesota P, 1988.

Markfield, Wallace. "Three First Novels." *Commentary* April 1950: 390-92.

Martin, Wallace. *Recent Theories of Narrative*. Ithaca: Cornell UP, 1986.

May, Elaine Tyler. *Homeward Bound: American Families in the Cold War Era*. New York: Basic, 1988.

May, Lary, ed. *Recasting America: Culture and Politics in the Age of the Cold War*. Chicago: Chicago UP, 1989.

Mcrivalc, Patricia. "The Flaunting of Artifice in Vladimir Nabokov and Jorge Luis Borges." *Wisconsin Studies in Literary Criticism* 8.2 (1967): 295-309.

Miller, Arthur. "On Social Plays." Introduction to *A View from the Bridge*. New York: Viking, 1955.

Miller, Nancy K. "Emphasis Added: Plots and Plausibilities in Women's Fiction." In *The New Feminist Criticism*. Ed. Elaine Showalter. New York: Pantheon, 1985: 339-360. Reprinted from *PMLA* 96 (1981).

Miller, Wayne Charles. *An Armed America: American Military Novel: A History of the American Military Novel*. New York: New York UP, 1970.

Millgate, Michael. *American Social Fiction: James to Cozzens*. Edinburgh: Oliver and Boyd, 1964.

Miner, Madonne M. *Insatiable Appetites: Twentieth Century American Women's Best Sellers.* Contributions in Womens Studies 48. Westport, CT: Greenwood, 1984.

Modleski, Tania. "The Disappearing Act." *Signs: Journal of Women in Culture and Society* 5 (1980): 435-48.

–––. *Loving with a Vengeance: Mass-Produced Fantasies for Women.* Hamden, CT: Archon, 1982.

Nell, Victor. *Lost in a Book: The Psychology of Reading for Pleasure.* New Haven: Yale UP, 1988.

Nelson, Richard. Review of *The First Man in Rome,* by Colleen McCullough. *Minneapolis Star Tribune* 7 October 1990: f11.

Norris, Christopher. *Deconstruction: Theory and Practice.* London: Methuen, 1982.

Oakley, J. Ronald. *God's Country: America in the Fifties.* 1986. New York: Dembner, 1990.

O'Connor, Frank. *The Lonely Voice: A Study of the Short Story.* Cleveland: World, 1963.

O'Donnell, Patrick. *John Hawkes.* Twayne Author Series, ed. Warren French. Boston: G.K. Hall, 1982.

Ohmann, Richard. "The Shaping of the Canon: U.S. Fiction: 1960-1975." *Critical Inquiry* 10.1 (1983): 199-223.

Paglia, Camille. "Ninnies, Pedants, Tyrants, and Other Academics." *New York Times Book Review* 5 May 1991: 1+.

–––. and Neil Postman. "She Wants her TV! He Wants His Book!" *Harper's* March 1991: 44+.

Parnell, Paul. "The Sentimental Mask." *PMLA* 78 (1963): 529-35.

Parsons, Nicholas. *The Book of Literary Lists.* New York: Facts on File, 1987.

Piper, William Bowman. "Tristram Shandy's Tragicomical Testimony." *Criticism* 3.3 (1961): 171-85.

Podhoretz, Norman. "Gibbsville and New Leeds: The America of John O'Hara and Mary McCarthy." *Commentary* 21 (1956): 269-73.

Postman, Neil. *Amusing Ourselves to Death: Public Discourse in the Age of Show Business.* New York: Penguin, 1986.

Potter, David. *People of Plenty: Economic Abundance and American Character.* 1954. Chicago: U of Chicago P, 1965.

Pratt, Mary Louise. *Toward a Speech-Act Theory of Literary Discourse.* Bloomington: Indiana UP, 1977.

Propp, Vladimir. *Morphology of the Folktale.* 2nd ed. Trans. Laurence Scott. Austin: U of Texas P, 1968.

Pryce-Jones, Alan. "The Fabulist's Worlds: Vladimir Nabokov." In Balakian and Simmons, 63-78.

Radford, Jean, ed. *The Progress of Romance: The Politics of Popular Fiction*. London: Routledge and Kegan Paul, 1986.

Radway, Janice. *Reading the Romance: Women, Patriarchy and Popular Literature*. Chapel Hill: U of North Carolina P, 1984.

Redman, Ben Ray. "Decline and Fall of the Whodunit." *Saturday Review* 31 May 1952: 8+.

Reich, Charles. *The Greening of America*. New York: Random, 1970.

Reutlinger, D.P. "*The Cannibal*: The Reality of Victim." *Critique* Fall 1963: 30-37.

Rice, J. M. Review of *Circle of the Day*, by Helen Howe. *Commonweal* 16 June 1950: 254.

Roberts, Michele. "Write, She Said." In Radford 221-255.

Roberts, Thomas J. *An Aesthetics of Junk Fiction*. Athens, GA: U of Georgia P, 1990.

Rolo, Charles. "This Man's Army." Review of *From Here to Eternity*. *Atlantic Monthly* March 1951: 83-84.

Robinson, Forrest G. *Having it Both Ways: Self-Subversion in Western Popular Classics*. Albuquerque: U of New Mexico P, 1993.

Root, Robert L. *The Rhetorics of Popular Culture: Advertising, Advocacy, and Entertainment*. New York: Greenwood, 1987.

Rosenberg, Bernard, and David M. White, eds. *Mass Culture: The Popular Arts in America*. Glencoe, IL: Free, 1957.

Rosenberg, Betty. *Genreflecting: A Guide to Reading Interests in Genre Fiction*. Littleton, CO: Libraries Unlimited, 1982.

Rovit, Earl. "The Fiction of John Hawkes: An Introductory View." *Modern Fiction Studies* 10 (1964): 150-62.

Ruthven, K.K. *Myth*. The Critical Idiom 31. London: Methuen, 1976.

Salomon, Roger B. *Desperate Storytelling: Post-Romantic Elaboration of the Mock-Heroic Mode*. Athens, GA: U of Georgia P, 1987.

Scheman, Naomi. "Though This Be Method, Yet There Is Madness in It: Paranoia and Liberal Epistemology." In *Engenderings: Constructions of Knowledge, Authority, and Privilege*. New York: Routledge, 1993: 75-105. Also in *A Mind of One's Own: Feminist Essays on Reason and Objectivity*, eds. L. Anthony and C. Witt. Boulder, CO: Westview, 1992.

Schott, Webster. "James Purdy: American Dreams." *Nation* 23 March 1964: 300-302.

– – –. "Vision of a Nightmare." *Nation* 2 September 1961: 122-23.

Schulz, Max F. *Radical Sophistication: Studies in Contemporary Jewish-American Novelists.* Athens, OH: Ohio UP, 1969.

Scott, Nathan A., Jr. "The Dark and Haunted Tower of Richard Wright." Hemenway 72-87. Reprinted from *Black Expression*, ed. A. Gayle, Jr. New York: Weybright, 1969.

Searle, John R. *Expression and Meaning: Studies in the Theory of Speech Acts.* Cambridge: Cambridge UP, 1979.

– – –. *Speech Acts: An Essay in the Philosophy of Language.* Cambridge: Cambridge UP, 1969.

Sinfield, Alan, ed. *Society and Literature 1945-1970: The Context of English Literature.* New York: Holmes E. Meier, 1983.

Sisk, John P. "American Best Sellers." *Commonweal* 11 July 1958: 373-75.

– – –. "Keats' American Dream." *America* 12 March 1960: 706-708.

"Slipped Disk." Review of *Man in the Gray Flannel Suit. Time* 18 July 1955: 102.

Smith, Barbara Herrnstein. "Contingencies of Value." *Critical Inquiry* 10 (1983): 1-35. Also in *Contingencies of Value: Alternative Perspectives for Cultural Theory.* Cambridge, MA: Harvard UP, 1988.

Soule, George. "Must a Novelist Be an Artist?" *Carleton Miscellany* 5.2 (1964): 92-98.

Stevenson, David L. "James Jones and Jack Kerouac: Novelists of Disjunction." In Balakian and Simmons, 193-212.

– – –. "Styron and the Fiction of the Fifties." *Critique* 3.3 (1960): 47-58.

Sullivan, Richard. Review of *The Healer* by Frank Slaughter. *Chicago Tribune* 23 January 1955, 3.

Susman, Warren with Edward Griffin. "Did Success Spoil the United States? Dual Representations in Postwar America." In L. May, 19-37.

Sutherland, John. *Bestsellers: Popular Fiction of the Seventies.* London: Routledge and Kegan Paul, 1981.

Taylor, Helen. "*Gone with the Wind*: The Mammy of Them All." In Radford, 113-136.

Tompkins, Jane. *Sensational Designs: The Cultural Work of American Fiction 1790-1860.* New York: Oxford UP, 1985.

Waldmeir, Joseph J. *American Novels of the Second World War.* The Hague: Mouton, 1969.

– – –. "Only an Occasional Rutabaga: American Literature since 1945." *Modern Fiction Studies* 15 (1969-70): 467-83.

Walsh, Jeffrey. *American War Literature 1914 to Vietnam.* New York: St. Martins, 1982.

Watt, Ian. *The Rise of the Novel: Studies in Defoe, Richardson, and Fielding.* 1957. Berkeley: U of California P, 1964.

Weales, Gerald. "Life on Madison Avenue." Review of *Man in the Gray Flannel Suit*, by Sloan Wilson. *Commonweal* 26 August 1955: 525-26.

Weeks, Edward. "The Young Marines": Review of *Battle Cry* by Leon Uris. *Atlantic Monthly* August 1953: 82+.

Whyte, William H., Jr. *The Organization Man.* Garden City, NY: Doubleday, 1956.

Wicker, Brian. *The Story-Shaped World: Fiction and Metaphysics: Some Variations on a Theme.* Notre Dame, IN: U of Notre Dame P, 1975.

Wolfe, Tom. "Stalking the Billion-Footed Beast." *Harper's* November 1989: 44-56.

Zipes, Jack David. *Breaking the Magic Spell: Radical Theories of Folk and Fairy Tales.* London: Heinemann, 1979.

INDEX

Lightning Source UK Ltd.
Milton Keynes UK
27 November 2009

146739UK00001B/108/P